The College of Saint Scholastica

Bequest of

Bishop Paul F. Anderson
1917-1987

Fifth Bishop of Duluth
1969-1983

Library May 1987

EROS
REDISCOVERED

EROS

REDISCOVERED

Restoring Sex to Humanity

Allen

by Leslie Paul

ASSOCIATION PRESS / NEW YORK

EROS REDISCOVERED

First American Edition 1970

© *Leslie Paul* 1969

Association Press, 291 Broadway, New York, N.Y. 10007

Standard Book Number: 8096-1785-4

Library of Congress Catalog Card Number: 75-132394

Printed in the United States of America

To Paul and Sue Wilkinson with love

ACKNOWLEDGMENTS

I wish gratefully to acknowledge my thanks to the publishers, authors and executors, whose names follow, for permission to publish extracts from the works listed:

Messrs. Little, Brown and Company and Dr. Donald J. Holmes for quotation from *The Adolescent in Psychotherapy* by Donald J. Holmes: Messrs. Victor Gollancz Ltd. for quotations from *Reminiscences of Affection* and *My Dear Timothy* by Victor Gollancz, also for quotation from *Male and Female* by Margaret Mead: *Observer* and Mary Miles for quotation from her article "Painful First Love" in the *Observer,* July 30, 1967: to the *Observer* also for quotation from the article "Revolution by Computer" by Dr. N. S. Sutherland in the *Observer,* April 9, 1967: Messrs. Geoffrey Bles Ltd. and H. M. Burton for quotation from *There was a Young Man* by H. M. Burton: The Princeton University Press for quotation from Vol. I, *Either/Or* by Sören Kierkegaard, translated by W. Lowrie, D. F. and L. M. Swenson (copyright 1944 by Princeton University Press): Messrs. J. M. Dent and Mr. Charles Mountford for quotation from *Brown Men and Red Sand* by Charles Mountford: Tandem Books and Charles Hamblett and Jane Deverson for quotation from *Generation X* by Charles Hamblett and Jane Deverson: The Viking Press and Robert O. Ballou for quotation from *The Viking Portable World Bible,* edited by Robert O. Ballou: Messrs. William Heinemann Ltd., Laurence Pollinger Ltd. and the Estate of the late Mrs. Frieda Lawrence for quotation from *Lady Chatterley's Lover* by D. H. Lawrence: *The Christian Century* and Earl H. Brill for quotation from "Sex is Dead," copyrighted 1969 Christian Century Foundation and reprinted by permission from August 3, 1966 issue of *The Christian Century: Kenyon Review* and C. H. Rolph for quotation from the article "The Literary Censorship in England" by C. H. Rolph in Vol. XXIX, June 1967: Messrs. J. M. Dent and Sons Ltd. for quotation from *Portuguese Voyages 1498–1663,* edited by Charles David Ley: to the Editors of *Life* and Richard Schickel for the quotation from Richard Schickel's review of *The Fox* in the issue of May 13, 1968, reprinted by permission of the Sterling Lord Agency: Messrs. Anthony Blond Ltd. and Jean Genet for quotation from *Our Lady of the Flowers* by Jean Genet: The Seabury Press and Richard Hettlinger for quotation from *Living with Sex: The Student's Dilemma* by Richard Hettlinger: to Messrs. André Deutsch and Norman Mailer for quotation from *An American Dream* by Norman Mailer: Messrs. Nelson and Gillian Freeman for quotation from *The Undergrowth of Literature* by Gillian Freeman.

Some of the themes developed in *Eros Rediscovered* received a preliminary discussion in my *Nature into History* (Faber, 1957), particularly in Chapters 4, 5 and 8. But there the interest was in the development of a philosophy of history rather than in exploring human sexual discipline specifically.

CONTENTS

Acknowledgments   7
1. THE BEAST AND THE GOD   11
2. SEX AND THE SPECIES   27
3. INCEST AND THE BIRTH OF MORALITY   38
4. SEX AS THE GIFT OF SOCIETY   48
5. SEXUAL ALIENATION AND
   TECHNOLOGY   70
6. SEX AS AN IRRELEVANCE   93
7. THE FAMILY AS THE MASTER
   PATTERN   100
8. THE SEXUAL LATENCY OF THE CHILD   110
9. THE PRIVATIZATION OF HUMAN LIFE   119
10. THE DISTANCING OF THE BODY   131
11. "INTER FAECES ET URINAM
    NASCIMUR"   140
12. SEX IN A DISINTEGRATING CULTURE   151
    Notes   176
    Index   187

CHAPTER one

THE BEAST AND
THE GOD

1

    Man, Aristotle said, is by nature a political animal. Of course he was wrong. Man is by nature an *animal*. If he is at the same time political that is the consequence of something else. To be paradoxical, it is not by nature but by *his* nature that he is political. Perhaps we should amend the saying: Man is by his social nature a political animal. It takes us out of the biological, but not much farther. Many species of animals are social in the complete sense that if one extracts the mature individual animal from its society, it perishes. Some are political. Their societies are not symbiotic huddles for mutual warmth, comfort and support like murmurations of starlings or herds of antelopes, but orderly, hierarchical structures through the mysterious authority of which the role of the individual is determined. The individual's survival is entirely dependent on the fulfillment of its predetermined contribution to the superior community.

    Of course Aristotle did not mean that man was a political animal in the sense that he was political in virtue of his animality, but quite the contrary. He was expressing the paradox: man is political against his animality. He is given his animality; he has his politics to make for himself. True, his animality gives him a societal role. But that role never totally determines his politics; it is merely the raw material his politics makes use of, and down the vistas of history sculptures into such astonishing shapes.

Perhaps one should amend Aristotle in another way and say, "Man is by nature a cultural animal." The word "politics" has a more restrictive meaning to the modern world than it had to his. All the same, "political" has a value not immediately apparent in "cultural." It evokes the hurly-burly, the rough day-to-day struggle for power. It illuminates the war of factions in tribe, city, nation and the ruthless ambitions of individuals. It presents to us the bloody world of Macbeth rather than the gentle reflectiveness of *Elegy in a Country Churchyard*. What Aristotle also means is this cultural dimension which man adds to his animality, a dimension he lives with such passion and suffering, in which he is "either a beast or a god."

A generation ago Professor V. Gordon Childe wrote a book called *Man Makes Himself*,[1] described exultantly on the blurb as "an authoritative history of the rise of civilization and of the means by which man has achieved mastery of his environment." The pithy title is all, and nothing could better express what this introduction is trying to say. Beyond his animality, man has everything to do for himself. When we speak of politics and culture, of science and technology, of art and civilization too, we speak of the dimension in which nothing is given to man but in which "man makes himself." It is a theme to which I shall recur again and again in the pages that follow.

I first explored this theme in a socioanthropological way in *Nature Into History*.[2] I was driven to it as a philosopher by the uncritical assumptions of so many evolutionary scientists and thinkers that human history was "just" a continuation of biological evolution. It seemed to me then and it seems to me still far too glib and unreflective a presupposition, made no easier to elucidate by those resounding contemporary dogmas that "man is in charge of his own evolution" or "in man evolution has become conscious of itself." It is logically the case that these must be statements impossible to verify or to put into a context in which they would be self-justifying. It was concern with this superficiality which urged me into a study of the differences between the closed realm of nature and the open dimension of history. For the open dimension, the word "evolution" was far too empty and overworked a term to bear the weight of all that had happened historically and all that was going to happen. There was no intention to deny that the evolution of species had taken place, only to question what the term meant when transferred loosely to human history where nothing is given and "man makes himself."

I probed as far as I could into that mysterious point of disjunction (a point that could stretch for thousands of years) where man takes himself out of the natural cycle and becomes a being not only of nature but of history, a being not only subject to biological controls, but in thrall to cultural "norms." More, a being who had to subject his biological nature, his animality, to ends and purposes beyond that nature.

It was clear that the problem of sexuality was critical for that self-transformation. It is for this reason that *Nature Into History* serves as an introduction to this essay on man's sexuality. Every man knows that his sexual drives have a certain autonomy within him: he does not himself wholly control his lusts and aversions. The timing and direction of his longings are often beyond him. Creatures of other species live somnambulistically within their procreative cycle. External circumstances permitting, it is that which is completely in control. It is impossible to conceive of man living somnambulistically his sexual cycle and at the same time the free, open dimension of history of which self-awareness and decision making are the preconditions. The price of conscious movement in the dimension of history is self-consciousness, and central to that is sexual self-consciousness. So for me the point of human explosion out of nature into history was that point at which man became aware of birth and death, time and space, and author of responsible deeds and moral decisions. It is the point too at which he had to take over and transform his sexuality. He ceases to be a creature of the dream time. The somnambulistic cycle is over.

Even so, one has to avoid oversimplification. Perhaps no human victory is complete. Perhaps every new generation, whatever its technological and cultural heritage, has to make its own struggle to be human. Every growing child comes in puberty to the moment of total sexual self-awareness with the consequences of which it now knows for certain it must live to the end of its days. It is a transformed being. It is the discovery of what it is to be, in Aristotelian terms, a sexual animal and a political man, a beast and a god.

Man must always be a two-dimensional being, living biologically and culturally simultaneously and in nothing is this more apparent than in his social life where the tension between the simple biological impulse and its elaborate cultural fulfillment in terms socially approved, is eternal. It is the price paid for his election to live in the dimension of history. This book is concerned with that theme, with how man regards his sex, how he contains and enjoys it within his moral and social frameworks. It is specially concerned with what sex means at this moment of history in our unique technological society, which, as so many have observed, is transforming everything, even sexual values, even (it is not improbable) sex itself. It is the Nietzschean moment of the transvaluation of all values.

2

What vanishes first in this perspective is sex in its simplicity. There are a number of contemporary doctrines of sex into which the notion of simplicity enters. At some of them we shall look in detail. It is enough to mention here the dream of a vanished golden age of sex to be found in primitive peoples or in antiquity, where nakedness was taken for granted and no puritanical taboos stood in the way of the sexual enjoyment of whatever couples wished to come together. It is present in all dreams of paradisal societies located in past ages, remote places, future Utopias.

A more down-to-earth philosophy is that which argues that sex *is* simple and that our anxieties are the result of ignorance, misin-

formation, social prejudice. Sex is an appetite, made to be gratified
like any other appetite. A gland fills: sooner or later it has to be
emptied, why not empty it? And why involve morals in that simple,
natural necessity? Why bother? Mary Quant (in an interview, *The
Guardian,* October 10, 1967) said of the young, "They've got sex
in perspective, they're not hung up on it any more, it's not difficult,
they take it or leave it alone. They're the best lot that ever happened." There is a kind of hatred of fuss or complication or taboo
which strikes me as compulsively the modern attitude, particularly
among young people. One even discerns a determination not simply
to see sex this way, but to "have sex" this way.[3]

A formidable group of young people obviously desire a promiscuous society, almost with indifference to the consequences which
follow, children, linear polygamy or concubinage, the dismissal of
deep and lasting personal relations, the general familial consequences. With loathing, they contract out of "family," if not society.

There is no doubt that this attitude is deeply influenced by social
and technological developments. Mary Quant remarked in that
interview I have mentioned that the girls had the pill, they were
the sex in charge, "They, and they only, can decide to conceive."
The pill, other contraceptive devices, and abortion laws and the
moral climate free sexual intercourse from many of its personal
consequences. The view is encouraged that sexual activity need have
no consequences, that it is so to speak an end in itself.

Not simply an engineering view of sex would appear to promote
this, but that vulgarized Freudian view that repression, particularly
sexual repression, is bad for body and psyche.

3

The decision (mostly but not wholly of the young) that sex
is an uncomplicated thing (or would be if the views of the old and
impotent were got rid of) flies in the face of a mass of psychological
evidence about the difficulty of achieving normal sexual development, emotional maturity, or happiness between sexual partners.
It would appear also to contradict the evidence about sexual devia-

tions and perversions, unless these too are accepted as legitimate and therefore as norms in themselves. There is a Kinsey view of sex to which this is appropriate. (The norm is simply what you do). But it does not only appear that scientific evidence is set aside—almost the whole of that contemporary literature, much of it the best fiction, concerned with the difficulties and frustrations of loving relations, genital relations, the pursuit of partners, the pain of rejection, almost all this literature is set aside in favor of the simple view. Alas, it is impossible to think in terms either of a sweet natural sex or an unimportant mechanical sex denied to the young by an unnatural society. The terms "natural" and "unnatural" have no meaning in this context. What is meaningful is what society does with the sex of its members, how it copes, or else fails as a society.

We have to put sexual encounters into the context of all our human relations in order to discover the magnitude of sociosexual problems. Jean-Paul Sartre speaks time and time again of the violence of the encounter between human beings. He summarized it in the aphorism "Hell is my neighbor." No human relations are *easy*. At their most placid and undemanding they are probably at their least meaningful. We get on very well with the neighbor we hardly ever see or the park keeper raking the leaves who nods to us as we pass by. It is the wife across the table or the casual adolescent son coming down late to breakfast full of unspoken criticism, or the bullying boss who riles us. Just in the degree that relations with others could be most rewarding and most fulfilling they so often prove unendurable. In the hands of Jean-Paul Sartre the I-Thou of Martin Buber becomes I *versus* Thou. The Other who stands over against me is the one I dread. He is the one who *sees* me, although in my own estimation I am the one who should be doing the seeing. I look out at the world and measure it up, deciding what the objects in it are and what they mean to me, dividing them into the categories, neutral, friendly, hostile. My stare dominates the world and I enjoy my solipsistic supremacy, or so I would wish, but the Other is the one who comes over my horizon and includes me in *his* stare. By his look I am reduced to an object in his field of vision. I don't exist for myself any longer but only as an object in his perspective. This is not only disconcerting but a cause of fear and apprehension, and I cannot enter his mind and decide what his presence bodes for me. That other perspective is beyond my comprehension, it is alien and alienates me, even from myself. This is how the prisoner must feel, trapped and under the jailer's glare in a Kafka-like authoritarian maze he cannot manipulate.

Jean-Paul Sartre has many eloquent ways of describing how the stare of the Other limits, even strips me, sees through me and deprives me of my presence of mind. It forces me to be present to him. The Other robs me of my incognito. He is the flow of the world toward another's world which I am powerless to arrest. When I am full of shame the Other is that immense presence, a kind of public awareness (like that which someone feels who is committing privately an evil deed which he suddenly discovers is under full public gaze) "which supports this shame and embraces it on every side."

Despite the existentialist extravagance of language, Jean-Paul Sartre is speaking here to real but often minimized human situations, to the difficulty of contacts and relations between human beings, to the fact that many—ought one even to say all?—relations display elements of tension or aggression, of withdrawal or avoidance, of lying, guilt or complicity. These necessary but gritty, raw-edged relations run through all situations and encounters, in endless variation. They do not need a specifically sexual element. They occur without that in board rooms and chambers of deputies, in trade union meetings and mothers' unions, in schools and common rooms, on factory floors and in ships' forecastles. They are an inevitable part of the nonsexual human nexus, and the world's social and political struggles (race, class, culture) are mostly about them. Desmond Morris in *The Naked Ape* [4] spells it all out for us in the primate gestures and grimaces of domination or submission, placation or aggression and in the grooming techniques which we in our civilized society still use as frequently, as unconsciously and more elaborately than apes as means of placation. Intersex relations add another dimension, one moreover triggered at the depths of our being, out of a biological inheritance and a psychical structure coming from racial millennia of which the ordinary unreflective man can hardly ever be more than momentarily aware. A sexual encounter carries the burden of the Sartrian relationship of a one to the Other, plus all that is demanded physically and spiritually by sex itself.

If we cannot rationalize and harmonize our nonsexual relations, which are after all those most open to reason and common sense, it is hardly likely that we shall at a blow come to either a sexual maturity or a sexual innocence. Indeed the sexual life itself has to struggle for its rights and its outlets in the labyrinth of the nonsexual, and becomes entangled with it, so that a simple division between the sexual and nonsexual is hardly possible in modern life. I am not dealing in figures of speech only. The boy and youth who must contain, disguise and even disavow his sexual urges from high school to the end of university days for the sake of his studies and his social acceptance is a case in point. So too is the sex deviant who is never permitted the open display or even private enjoyment of his particular sexual obsession, and must deny its existence even to himself.

It is not only in this negative sense that I see the interrelation between the sexual and the nonsexual. Man in his primitive state is a hunter; in his civilized state an acquisitive animal. There is plenty of anthropological evidence that he was a woman-stealer; in some primitive societies he still is. We have to recognize that he is a sexual as well as an economic predator, and for success in this he needs cunning, skill, patience and insight into the lives of his human victims just as much as into the animals he hunts. The stare of the Other can be the predatory stare of the *sexual* Other. But the predator knows better than the innocent of heart how to conceal the stare. He does not blush like his victims. The Mary Quant girl with her provocative crotch [5] not only invites the comradely questioning look of her contemporary, but the stare her eyes do not engage, the stare of the rapist, eyes before which they may fall in fear. No woman passes through life without experiencing the penetrating glance which strips her of personality (and clothes) and turns her into a thing, an erotic assembly of limbs, which the predator is already imaginatively exploiting.

In this context we might examine a piece of nineteenth-century

writing which explores with the utmost romanticism the role of
sexual predator—"Diary of the Seducer" in Kierkegaard's *Either/
Or*. It is the story of the intrigue of a young man-about-town, probably in his thirties, directed at the seduction of a sixteen-year-old
girl he has accidentally met on his walks through the town. He does
not know her and so must worm his way into the circle in which
she moves and then must tantalize her by paying court to everyone
but her. He even contrives to get a friend affianced to her knowing
the engagement must break down and that he will catch her on the
rebound. He is hot and cold by turn and turn about to confuse her
and draw her simpleness on, and engages her in an arch correspon-
dence to mystify her and detach her from her moral innocence.
And it is she who must, by his contriving, break this engagement
too in order that she shall be alone and without defenses and he
without commitments. He has casual sex encounters with servant
girls along the route to the planned seduction. He sets out his
philosophy of sex in his diary.

Practically, I have reached the point where I desire nothing which is
not, in the strictest sense, freely given. Let common seducers use such
methods. What do they gain? He who does not know how to compass a
girl about so that she loses sight of everything which he does not wish
her to see, he who does not know how to poetize himself in a girl's feelings so that it is from her that everything issues as he wishes it, he is
and remains a bungler; I do not begrudge him his enjoyment. A bungler
he is and remains, a seducer, something one can by no means call me.
I am an aesthete, an eroticist, one who has understood the nature and
meaning of love, who believes in love and knows it from the ground up,
and only makes the private reservation that no love affair should last
more than six months at the most, and that every erotic relationship
should cease as soon as one has had the ultimate enjoyment. . . . To
poetize oneself into a young girl is an art, to poetize oneself out of her,
is a masterpiece. Still, the latter depends essentially upon the first.[6]

This philosopher of one-night stands (in "one-night cheap ho-
tels"?) gets his night of rapture. Byronically, he laments that it
could not be longer. Why could not the sun stand still? Then, brutally:

Still, it is over now, and I hope never to see her again. When a girl has given away everything, then she is weak, then she has lost everything; for a man guilt is a negative moment, for a woman it is the value of her being. Now all resistance is impossible, and only as long as that is present is it beautiful to love; when it is ended there is only weakness and habit. I do not wish to be reminded of my relation to her . . . I will have no farewell . . . nothing is more disgusting to me than a woman's tears.[7]

What is so revealing in this calculated exploitation is the utter bad faith of the seducer whether in a common or garden, or in an existentialist sense of bad faith. Everything is played according to the elaborate courtship rules of a society we should delight in calling Victorian. Not a word is said out of place, not a letter is blameworthy. By a masterly manipulation of the feelings of the young girl, she is brought to will, and long for, her own seduction. Outwardly correct, inwardly everything smells of falsity and hypocrisy. It is the kind of story that makes critics ask for more open sexual relations. But when we do meet the same kind of predator in our less polite but more permissive society—in the pages of Nabokov's *Lolita* or Golding's *Free Fall*—the stench of corruption is just as strong.

The philosophy of the young sex predator, the eternal "Alfie," was spelled out in what was recorded of a young Stoke-on-Trent layabout.[8]

I go out for rides with a friend and we usually latch on to some girls and get them to pay for us. We give them the full treatment. We say we're salesmen and that normally we have plenty of money and we're expecting some to come through. They pay for us a couple of times and then we drop them. We have a drink and go to a dance. They probably only spend ten shillings and they get a free ride in the car. We let them off light. . . . I take out two or three girls a week. I'm not serious about them and I'm not interested in marriage—too many ties. I find girls are usually willing to sleep with me, it's just a matter of wanting them bad enough. But I don't see them regularly. I smooth them over the first date. I take her out and we neck and I judge what she's like, whether she's hot stuff. If she is I take her out again and sleep with her. If I meet her in the street after that I'd say "hello" but that would be the end of it. If I got a girl pregnant I wouldn't marry her. After all, it takes two, doesn't it? If that ever happened I'd be miles away—in South America, I hope.

4

In considering sexuality so far we have remained within the realm of legitimate intercourse. One cannot pursue it very far before we discover lust merging into cruelty, cruelty into frenzy. Krafft-Ebing and a score of others have documented sexual activity in its demonic aspects. It took a novelist to speak of it as an element in the makeup of quite ordinary persons. James Baldwin, in a short story, "Going to Meet the Man," [9] tells of the collective lynching of a Negro by white countryfolk in broad daylight, an act committed in an ecstasy of bloodlust. A little white boy is taken to witness the man's destruction. The boy, Jesse, is lifted onto his father's shoulders to share the scene with the bright excited crowd gathered smiling and in their best clothes as to a Fourth of July picnic. The first act was an almost ritual castration, mutilation, after which the crowd went berserk. When all was over, the happy people dispersed to their farms to bake their bread and pies, and iron their clothes for Sunday church and chapel. The boy "felt that his father had carried him through a mighty test, had revealed to him a great secret which would be the key to his life forever."

Such frenzied cruelty and lust reveals to us as nothing else can the fearful complexities of the human heart—"The fury and the mire of human veins." It builds its own horrors and dread around the acts of sexual intercourse on which it then feeds to the point of the overthrow of every restraint, every counsel of humanity. Alas for the distance this places men from the sweet, simply natural acts of sex of the reformers! It does not appear that any human faculty is quite so corruptible.

There are other aspects of sex, which pertain more to comedy. No analysis of sex in contemporary society is worthwhile which does not see sex as a surrogate for the nonsexual passions, as well as a commodity which fetches a market. In fact one has the task of reversing the trend of thinking of the major part of a century which has shown sex as permeating, coloring every human activity from infancy on. Everything was the vehicle of sex, everyone said. But is it true? To show the reverse, the fate of the sexual at the hands of the nonsexual in human life, will be as illuminating. It has to be added though that the supremacy of the nonsexual has been *unconsciously* the motive of many agitators for sexual reform. Free sex from the straitjacket of convention, the tyranny of puritanism, the life denial of Christianity, and make it as easy and as unshocking as turning on the tap for a drink of water, has been the plea of many reformers in this century. To what end? To place it under the control of reason and contraceptives, to give it a placid, accepted and non-interfering role in our daily lives, has been the customary answer, which in a way is to propose to unsex society.

It cannot be argued that, even on the reforming side, a single view of sex has emerged in the course of the century. If one studies Krafft-Ebing's classical *Psychopathia Sexualis,* then it is hard to surface from his innumerable cases without the sense of sex as a clinical pathology. With Freud too the pathology of sex seems more important than the normality of sex, if indeed we can discover what the normality is. Perhaps there is no normality except a statistical one. The Kinsey view of sex would appear to be just that. Kinsey studies sexual activity statistically, across the whole range from bestiality and sodomy, and upward from childhood. There are sexual acts; their typicality or normality derive from a statistical mean rather than a moral principle. If one moves over to de Sade, whose ascendancy in those days is a striking commentary on the range of sexual activity society is prepared to contemplate, then for his philosophy non-sex would be the disease, the sign of a male impotence, a failure to act out the essential predatory role which nature demands and justifies.

Over against all the philosophies one can put the engineering view of sex, which hands it over to the technologists. They provide means for its control or reorganization. There are fertility pills and contraceptive pills, sterilization techniques, drugs to retard puberty, hormones to alter the sexual balance, sperm banks, surgery to change the externals of sex. The technologists can grow a mouse fetus on the testicle of a living rat as easily as grafting a second head on a living dog, and with as little reverence—as though all that evolution has bequeathed us is a biological game for the ingenious nursery tribes of clever, unfeeling children. Here the brave new world that hath such men and women in it is already on us.

5

What I have said is not new. Down the ages, and I do not mean just Christian ages, men have recognized the uncontrollable, the demonic element in sexuality and sought to bring the whole of sexual life under control by every conceivable discipline— females were secluded like precious objects locked in safes, males sacrificed their virility to idols or fled society, breakers of the code were done to death, the words of sex almost dropped from speech in puritan communities.

Freud saw in this immense disciplinary effort the erection of the social superego. The social superego fed the private superego: together they sustained and enhanced each other's power until it seemed impossible that anything could break the sexual censorship. At attempts to do so private and social fears and angers mounted. We meet the tyrannical superego disciplining the whole of a society into an attitude toward sex we can only regard as total in some of Margaret Mead's and Malinowski's primitive societies, and in Old Testament Israel and Christian puritanism. It seems present today in the prudish Soviet Union. It was the hallmark of our own Victorian era in which guilt over sex was universal.

"We are commonly dressed, and commonly behave," William Golding wrote, "as if we had no genitalia." [10] This may be passing in our day. Certainly we are often uncommonly dressed and uncommonly behave. But it was absolute in Victorian days. The cold marble pudenda of statues had to be concealed, the bare legs of tables raised anxieties about suggestiveness, and men's starved eyes lighted up at the exposure of a stockinged female ankle. Indeed, women were expected to behave as if they had no legs either. Sex went furtively underground and when on July 8, 1885, William

Stead published the third and most horrifying of his revelations about the white slave market—about the ease with which little girls could be purchased for prostitution—London erupted. Men and boys flocked in thousands to the streets, bringing traffic to a standstill, rendering the police helpless. A mysterious power drove them toward the offices of the *Pall Mall Gazette* off the Strand as to the place of a new revelation or the execution of a king. It was a moment, almost, of revolution.

There is still to this day in Britain a sense of rebellion against the sexual repression of Victorian society. Though the society has been gone from us for the better part of a century, it is spoken of (and by the young) as though it died only yesterday, and was still the principal enemy. That is a tribute to its power in the creation, without a political tyranny, of a universal social and sexual discipline, which all institutions were partners in upholding. And it was this kind of society—not limited to Britain—which Freud thought of as civilization, and as hardly worth the candle. Its social superego seemed so life-denying that men would be better without it. Much of the liberating power of Freud's thought was just its daring in the face of the nineteenth-century conspiracy of sexual silence.

We are now at the point of farthest rebound from Victorian society. It is as positively rejected in laws and mores as it could be. The censorships have gone. The superego has ebbed away. But an impulsive rejection of restraints is not a new discovery so much as an abandonment of old psychosocial structures, with nothing perhaps to replace them. Sex is culturally omnipresent; indeed the literary arts seem to have no other compelling subject of discourse. The exploitation of sex is a vast and profitable capitalist enterprise. But a sense of what sex is about is missing. Its ubiquity contributes to rather than disperses the social aimlessness.

The Victorians were sure what sex was about and where its place was. It was about procreation and its lawful place was within marriage, and (something we forget) marriage and sex were judged to be at their finest within the context of romantic love and maternal devotion. And this lent style and structure (and that Forsyte stiffness) to the whole of life. It was not the *positive* element of Victorianism which was ignoble, but the price paid for it. But the alternative to Victorianism is not "a general mess of imprecision." That seems only a decision to have nothing where once there was something. And out of nothing, nothing comes. Every sociologist speaks of the disintegrating forms of contemporary cultures, of the anonymity and despair of great cities, the *anomie* of those deprived of meaningful personal relations or reduced to ciphers in technopolis, the emptiness of those who find themselves goalless and clueless in the face of uncontrollable forces. We are forced to see in the lives of urbanized man a desperate search for identity. I think we can also speak meaningfully of the search for sexual identity amidst collapsing psychosocial structures.

John Wilson is surely right in his seminal *Logic and Sexual Morality* [11] in saying that we ought to be able "to create something now sadly lacking; some sense of *style* in sexual relationships, as opposed to the present furtiveness, sordidity and tongue-tied lovemaking. The total lack of any adequate ritual or convention in these relationships itself bears witness to our failure to include them in our education; as in so many contexts, teenagers learn no conventions of behaviour from adults so that their own are naturally primitive and inarticulate." In fact, the blundering id takes over.

But though we know what John Wilson means, the ritualization and stylization of sexual relationships means much more than giving them a personal aesthetic satisfaction. That may simply increase sexual individuation and so the mounting sense of alienation from society. It means giving sexual relations a symbolic quality, and that is only possible if one is conscious in one's sexual life of what society or religion values and wills to promote. Then one is identified with the values of society and is even exalted by the sense of fulfilling them to the point of sacrifice. Again and again we witness this identification with society where themes like duty, honor, patriotism, national liberation are concerned. We have forgotten how life-enhancing that identification can be where love and sexual relationships are concerned. They will then stand for the way society regards and values sex; they will identify the couple with that social evaluation. An identity, not simply an entity, is forged. This is what the girl instinctively feels about the "white wedding." In it she is justified before the world. But in a way the world is justified in her.

But how can all this be sustained, except in a socially residual way, where no conventions of behavior are transmitted by adults? If they retreat (and they are retreating) then no social superego will be built up—and then there is no point in style. Style has no use. It contributes nothing to a society the mores of which are disintegrating. Style has no meaning *if it communicates nothing to society*. But it is not alone style which is missing but sexual identity in the sense of gender role. It appears sometimes that a permanent adolescence is being assumed in which everything is worth trying but nothing worth enduring.

If the search for sexual integrity is hard in a repressive society because so much of the sex of man is denied or hidden away, it is just as hard in the promiscuous society in which no discipline is demanded and the superego is pensioned off. Sexual integrity implies a struggle against both societies. Neither meets the human need for sexual activity which is generously fulfilling and which has a ritualized dignity and grandeur, beauty and delight. The one society, out of fear, seems to sacrifice everything to achieve silence, the other to throw away the love and the grandeur for the instant orgasm. There has to be a middle way.

CHAPTER two

SEX AND THE
SPECIES

1

      To ask what sex is, is almost as foolish as asking what time is. We understand what time is until we ask questions about it, we understand what sex is until we ask *what* it is. Time, in the sense of its progression and irreversibility, is the datum upon which our lives rest. Without it, they cannot be explained, but time itself, Kant notwithstanding, is not to be explained by our lives. Sex, too, is part of human givenness; as gender it is the governing principle of every individual life, which finds much, if not all, of the reason for its existence in it. People, down into the cradle, into the womb, are male or female. Potentialities, attitudes, appetites, satisfactions as well as physical forms, are determined by this basic division. So too are social contributions and opportunities. For the individual it is a givenness just as time is, and as irreversible.[1] No one chooses his or her own sex.

    Then, too, sex is magical; the power which draws opposite sexes together though not as irresistible as breathing is almost as irresistible as appetite. Where breathing is the *sine qua non* of the life of the breathing organism and is almost as unnoticed an activity as the beating of the heart or the circulation of the blood, sexual activity has no such inevitable status—therein lies its problem. Organisms continue to live even if deprived of it. For the male consort of the black widow spider or the praying mantis, coitus is death: the fertilized female proceeds to eat the male. If the male's survival is the point of the male life, sexual activity is a disaster. We know that chemical processes bring an animal or a bird to heat after latency. The chemical servicing of biological processes is not to be denied. But with birds in courtship display, a display close to aggression, there is a powerful visual, even aesthetic element, as a means of sexual recognition and acceptance, and of chemical or hormonic stimulation. The whole *attention* of the organism appears to be focally aroused on the sexual object. Sex is very much this total living attention and the subordination of all vital processes to its demands while they last. With the boys and girls on display in King's Road, Chelsea, on any Saturday, the engagement, the excitement, of the imagination too is complete. It is to this that some one pointed when he remarked, "Supposing the magic failed?" Physical appetites such as hunger, or spiritual ones such as the will-to-power, manifestly serve the ends of the individual organism. Sex too fulfills an organism, for it was for this it was created in its gender, but it fulfills it, raising to supreme heights of vitality, élan, joy, for ends firmly beyond the individual organism and sometimes destructive of it. Perhaps it was this that W. H. Auden meant when he wrote, "We are lived by powers we pretend to understand." [2]

Not only is sex, considered as gender, irreversible, but the sexual activities which follow from gender are by definition exclusive. The male or female experience is polar. It is the condition of its expression that the opposing experience cannot be enjoyed. Not even through the cultivation of sexual aberrations is any human being both male and female simultaneously or by alternation. Plato, in the *Symposium,* argued that every human being was only half a human being, excluded by his or her sex from the range of activity and understanding belonging to the other half. The description of woman as "man's better half" belongs to this intuition. Plato de-

scribed the human race as destined to a frantic search for whole-
ness or completion through the discovery of the appropriate sexual
partner. It is a description which fits the social behavior of men
and women as well as the subjective expectations of what will be
given to us by loving sex experiences. It is even a wry commentary
on human pretensions to self-sufficiency and self-fulfillment that
there is never one humanity but two, a male humanity and a female
humanity, each necessary to the other but incapable of standing
in the place of the other, and each penetrating the other, apart
from sexually, only infirmly in the imagination. This is a fundamental aspect of the human *mysterium*—that it is never a totality,
always a duality, and that it learns its own role in dialogue with its
opposing gender. Only the fact that gender is a datum, at which
one stares rather than with which one argues, accustoms us to
accepting it with such banality.

Of course what the sexual activity of the human, as well as of
other species, achieves biologically is easy to state. It achieves
reproduction, and the purpose of reproduction, speaking teleo-
logically, is survival. By the production of young, fully equipped
with the somatic forms and behavioral capabilities of their an-
cestors, the species is protected from the extinction which would
otherwise follow the death of its members. The higher the rate
of reproduction and the greater therefore the spread of the species, the greater the insurance against extinction. Reproduction
is the natural insurance against the death of the species and
compensation for individual death. Reproduction is not necessarily *sexual,* however; that is also to say it is *reproduction* which
is crucial, not the means by which it is achieved. There are
asexual forms of reproduction in such organisms as the amoeba,
which propagates by division, and yeast, which buds, and there
are parthenogenetic forms in greenfly and water fleas. Yet the
sexual mode of reproduction is the dominant one throughout species
and appears to arise as something imposed on reproduction, and
alien to it, a check on undisciplined growth. And this too has survival value. The reproduction of the species through union of individuals of opposing genders means the most constant re-sorting
of genetic variations consistent with the retention of the species-

form. It prevents too great a rigidity of types. The greater the range of variations the greater the possibility that some of them will have survival value: it perhaps is as simple as that.

One may put it another way and say that every individual organism is the bearer of a species-form, is committed to the exploitation of that form and to its transmission. When the mode of reproduction is sexual, then a social order is embryonically present. Male and female organs are necessary to each other, whether on the same parent body, as with certain plants, or as part of freely moving autonomous individuals. Sexual reproduction is not possible unless the sexes are *present* in *some* way to each other. When the intercourse involves prolonged bodily association then a dependence is created, recalling Plato's concept of incompleteness, which is socially as well as biologically exploited.

Of course what often appears to confront us in the natural world is a frenzy of reproduction as though a species had no other *raison d'être* except to reproduce itself to the limit of its powers. The annual cycle of the anthill or the beehive is a reproductive one. Everything in the way of food storage and the building of living accommodation is undertaken to enable a powerful nucleus of members to survive the winter hibernation. Then from spring to the hymeneal flight every resource is mustered and the highest degree of failure accepted, even total loss of the colonizing parties, year after year, in the effort to propagate the species. Almost as soon as this is done the hive or anthill begins once again to renew the cycle. Both these types of insect colony behave with what appears from the outside to be a complete single-mindedness in their pursuit of the reproductive cycle. Individual insects lose their sex for the sake of the greater fertility of the whole; the "whole" dictates the process. It is difficult to comprehend this organizationally except as a totalitarian acceptance of the priority of reproduction. But the fever of reproduction is not limited to insect colonies. Malthus made it the governing principle of human society. The growth of population would tend always to outstrip the growth of resources, he said, and equilibrium would only be restored again through war, pestilence and famine. (India today would appear to be a Malthusian test case.) Of course, famine and disease are governors of the population growth of *animal* species, and those somewhat dated Darwinian concepts "the struggle for existence" and "survival of the fittest" can serve in the animal kingdom as synonyms for human war. The point, however, is that all begins in the reproductive fever common to all species, including man.

Only quite recently, historically speaking, has the human species questioned its subjection to the reproductive cycle and begun the attempt to bring reproduction under control without using the Malthusian governors and without putting human fertility at risk. The whole world experiments with birth control, abortion and sterilization techniques. Sex in its magical sense, its gravitational pull, is not renounced (as in ascetic philosophies or cults such as that of Attis), but controls are placed upon its reproductive consequences. Where the pill and/or birth-control appliances are regularly used, an unwanted pregnancy becomes a remote possibility, an accident. Reproduction is placed at a "distance." As with artificial irrigation the control is theoretically absolute; either the tap is turned on or it isn't. If it is not, the disjunction of the reproductive capacity from sexual intercourse is complete. It is behind a wall without even Bottom's chink in it.

The theoretical possibility must exist that every mature male of a species can have fertile relations with every mature female of the same species and vice versa, or the term "species" is meaningless. The greatest promiscuity therefore might be held to offer the greatest evolutionary advantages in the reassembly of useful variations. In fact there are severe restraints on promiscuity among higher animals. Their young are born immature. They are always smaller than their parents, in some cases helpless, and without nurture and protection they would never survive to their own sexual maturity. For this reason maternal nurture is as imperative as gestation in the reproductive process—and paternal nurture too, almost as often (though the degree of this nurture varies extraordinarily; cuckoo adults, for instance, abandon their young). The female of a higher animal is, in gestation, in egg laying and hatching, in the feeding, warming, cleaning, caring for helpless young, not only physically burdened but vulnerable and exposed to natural predators. The protective and auxiliary role of the male progenitor is, if not irreplaceable, certainly advantageous in the birth and rearing stages of these young which are born immature.

We can say, then, that reproduction is not completed by birth, but continues socially for higher animals. It is not birth but the survival of the young to sexual maturity which is the goal, and this can only be accomplished familially, that is socially. Precisely this places a check on pure promiscuity. Any male of a species may procreate with any female of the same species and does so where the fertilized eggs are laid and abandoned. But familial obligations among certain mammals and birds make this intolerable: the female gives birth to and nurtures *her* young. The biological union of the mother with her young expresses itself proprietorially after birth. The housing of the young marsupial in its mother's pouch perfectly expresses this mutual proprietorship. The male progenitor, proprietorially linked with his mate or mates, extends this proprietorship to the young, though usually with less powerful a tie than the female's. Nevertheless some male birds will not only share in covering the eggs, and in feeding and cleaning the young, but will take over nurture if the hen bird is killed. The immaturity of the young creates *of necessity* a close bond between the parents and brings into being the family, the pack, the herd. In some species, mating is for life, so that promiscuity is abandoned for a stable biological and social union. Promiscuity in this evolutionary stage is a conspicuous disadvantage. The family unit with no identifiable male partner is simply shorthanded, endangered, incompetent —and still is in human society, whatever the reason for the loss of the male partner. Far below the human level then, sexual relations involve more than intercourse, which are no more than the first stage of a cycle which imposes familial duties, social structures, economic obligations—and even tyrannically so, as we have seen, for the cycle of mating and rearing continues without break till death for most creatures. Perhaps all this amounts to a truism. If so, it is a truism it is useful to restate at this moment of confusion over sex in human society.

2

Much of what has been said about birds and mammals is
true of the human situation, but it is not the whole truth. The
time scale is so different—one family, one lifetime, this is the
human average; not for man the frenzy of one or two broods every
year. Such a scale relaxes the reproductive tyranny though it does
not of itself abate sexual desire. Man, after all, is always "on heat."
Nevertheless man has time for other things and does much more
than procreate and raise families. He functions at other levels. He
builds cathedrals, makes airplanes, plays football, mines coal, goes
to war, fabricates languages and sciences, and destroys everything
as deliberately. Without severing his roots in the biological and
familial, he moves into the dimension of culture, civilization and
history. If there were no *moral* problems connected with sex there
would still be "problems" raised by man's determination to enjoy
the cultural dimension of human experience, for the cultural also
imposes its imperatives. If sex is not the only discipline or imperative in man's life, then he is subject to more than one discipline;
a tension inevitably possesses him. Shall he stay at home and raise
a family or go and fight in the wars? Shall he voyage with Drake
in the *Golden Hind* or marry the girl he loves and set up house?
Shall the only son of a noble family take monastic vows or keep
the line going? These are not moral situations but choices between
ends socially deemed equally good.

Then in this new dimension man lives *against* the biological and
reproductive in a manner inconceivable in any other species. He
deliberately risks his own life in exalted forms of "play"—mountain
climbing, exploration, even of space, motor racing—and so risks
his reproductive function. He makes war against his own species
and so destroys the reproductive powers of all who fall in battle—
fifty-nine million between 1820 and 1945 alone, as I pointed out
in an earlier book! [3] He will kill the young of his own species. The
slaughter of the innocents by Herod is not atypical; putting the male
young of a captured city to the sword or castrating them so that
they shall have no offspring to take revenge is a familiar enough

event in history. The extermination of a whole people,[4] the most significant event of twentieth-century history, shows that man's war against his own kind has simply grown more efficient with the passage of time. The use, or even the invention, of a bomb to kill millions and to endanger the fertility of the rest of the species is inexplicable, biologically speaking. Man has to justify it by reference to a higher principle than the biological or the reproductive— freedom, say, or defense, or hatred of communism or capitalism. I say this not to indulge in a moral tirade against our times (nothing is easier) but to show as sharply as possible how other values than the biological (even bad values) operate in human society and are constantly invoked to justify behavior which might be regarded as anti-reproductive, anti-evolutionary and inimical to survival. Viewed in this light, contraception, abortion, vows of celibacy, are means too of resisting the biological and bringing its consequences under the control of some specifically "human" principle—personal rights, social freedom, religious values. The biological knows nothing of personal rights; biologically there is only one "right" and that is to live, and that belongs more to a fetus than its begetters, for the fetus is the reproductive future while the parents who exterminate the fetus are already the reproductive past. Alas, human sexual dilemmas are not to be solved by an appeal to the biological or evolutionary. Unlike other species, man has passed the point where these are decisive for him, and what that means for man socially and morally is formidable, for (forward from some prehistoric point of decision) he must carry the burden of his own sexuality instead of being carried by it.

If a man chooses to become an engineer rather than a miner, a teacher rather than a solicitor, he may have some regrets but no seriously divided being because of his rejected choice. The teacher does not carry an inner "solicitorship" along with him, but the monk, living out his celibacy, does not extinguish his sexuality, but carries it rather as an impediment to his true vocation. By the same token, man in general, in seeking to live in the nonbiological, does not rid himself of the biological. His sex floods him the more powerfully in his imagination because it has to be brought under control or, in Freudian language, censored or repressed. There is therefore not only a struggle with the biological in society at large (a conflict not limited to sex but concerned also with the limits to the exposure of the body and its acts, and man's ambivalent relation to his own bodily presence), but in the heart of man himself. He cannot bear to be this natural sexual function *only,* but he cannot bear not to be a full man.

Sex as a problem, as giving rise to a conflict of disciplines, accords with much contemporary psychopathology, particularly Freud's, whose theories so profoundly color our culture. But it runs against one contemporary mythology of sex, that sex is only a pseudo-problem. This contemporary view (it is a significant commentary on our century that it is also a barrack-room view) would roughly run that sex is a bodily appetite like hunger and thirst. Just as it is dangerous not to eat or drink when you need to, so it is dangerous not to "have sex" when you want it. Repression does bodily or at any rate mental harm. Sex is a simple, expendable natural urge, the discharge of a gland, and to wrap it around with taboos, prohibitions, sanctions, is to make something necessary and pleasurable into an evil. Puritanical religion, at war with happiness and obsessed with sin, and jealous old people especially, are held to be responsible for the condemnation of sex in society. It is all there, unspoken, in the Mary Quant interview. This is a pragmatic, even engineering view of sex not unexpected in contemporary society, which believes everything manageable and finds it hard to conceive of anything except sex *repression* as either personally or socially dangerous.

All human appetites can be dangerous if they cannot be satisfied. A hungry man can be a dangerous man; a hungry people an invading people, as history shows. Yet it is also true that beyond a certain point the danger to others falls away: the hungry and thirsty cease to have the physical strength for acts of aggression; they die. The moment of greatest danger to others comes when they fear hunger, but yet hardly experience it, when hunger is still a psychological rather than a physical problem and they are strong. At this moment, the moment of defense of a future need, the problem is to know the extent of that need and what would satisfactorily meet it. The whole institution of property in physical things, in material goods, springs from this psychological anticipation of future wants and of devising the means to meet them. Which brings us to the quite opposite assumption from the engineering one about sex. Sexual appetite, like the property appetite in man, is no simple, direct human urge, like urinating, but something of infinite complication and capable of elaborate perversion and concerned deeply with its future consequences.

Cannibalism may be the product of protein hunger or of some religious imperative, but the danger—death to the eaten, degradation to the eater, insecurity to society—comes from the indulgence of the appetite, not from its suppression. A less archaic example is to be found in property rights. If what I have said above is true, the acquisition of property springs out of a perfectly healthy act of anticipation of future need, precisely the kind of thing which gives us our human scale, for there is no animal equivalent of General Motors or Prudential Insurance. But reformers have been telling us for nearly two hundred years that society is put in danger by the acquisitive instinct because the search for satisfaction for future needs moves over insensibly into a lust for property, whatever the shape it has, land, natural resources, rent, interest or profit. Society becomes the prey of the greedy and successful; the greedy and unsuccessful are the victims, and go to the wall. This appetite, whatever its natural origin in the urge of a beehive to store honey or of a squirrel to hoard nuts, or the cooperative impulse of a primatial hunting pack, has become for man a psychological dimension, worked over imaginatively and with calculation and gratified in a complex social environment. It has moved out of the dimension of a natural need clamoring to be satisfied, and forgotten once it has been, into something upon which both society (even the acquisitive society) and man himself in his inwardness impose strict conditions, stern disciplines. Even upon so direct and uncomplicated an act as meeting and greeting another person man is compelled to impose a personal and social discipline, accepting unconditionally the need for it, wrapping his reactions in gestures, too subtle for words, which arouse, accept, reject or smooth down the other. How much more inevitable therefore are the personal and social controls which have to be erected around the gratification of desires such as those for property, involving as they do the homes and the livelihood, the free passage and the personal well-being, even the life or death of others! I spoke earlier of the will-to-power as a spiritual appetite as real as any physical one. Almost certainly it is basically as protective in intention as the desire for property, and as physical in expression: the dominant male in the herd drives off the contender, the young animal fights to fulfill his role. Every contemporary society and all recorded history witness to the extent to which man has made over this will-to-power psychologically into a lust pursued for its own sake—and witness also to the contrary the quite unending human struggle to contain its exercise, to protect society from its consequences, to restrain its arbitrariness and to subject authority to law and law to common consent. I speak of the struggle for freedom or for the rule of law.

What we are saying then is that whatever the biological roots of human urges or appetites, the biological source is no guarantee of the value of their gratification or guide to their role. Everything of the biological in man is made over in the human psyche and in human society until the biological, or at least its expression, becomes the "gift" of society rather than the reverse. Human sexuality is no exception, rather the supreme exemplar. Neither the psyche nor society creates sex, but just as it is argued by Freud that the responsible human psyche is the product of an infantile tussle to bring sexual impulses under a psychological discipline, so it can be argued that human society itself arises out of the mastery (and exploitation) of the sexual for the sake of the social. But once this has been accomplished and society established as a basic human good, sexual activity, even sex itself, appears as the gift of society, and under the license of society. It becomes a power held on trust as, in many societies, property is on trust from society. Society gives and society can take away.

CHAPTER *three*

INCEST AND THE
BIRTH OF MORALITY

1

The meaning of the term "species" is, as I have explained, that where production is sexual, any male of the species can fertilize any female. There are physical and social limits to a general promiscuity among animal species. With man there are moral limits too. It is at the ethical we must look. David Hume picked up this point in *A Treatise of Human Nature* in his treatment of morals, saying, "I would fain ask anyone, why incest in the human species is criminal, and why the very same action, and the same relations in animals, have not the smallest moral turpitude and deformity? If it be answered, that this action is innocent in animals, because they have not reason to discover its turpitude; but that man, being endowed with that faculty, which *ought* to restrain him to his duty, the same action instantly becomes criminal to him." [1] But this he thought was arguing in a circle. For the turpitude to be discovered by reason, it had to exist independently of reason, that is prove to be an objective "fact" in a manner A. J. Ayer would approve. If there were such *facts* the animal kingdom "must be susceptible of all the same virtues and vices for which we ascribe praise and blame to human creatures." Because there is no such objective morality—no moral code exposed in things—vice and virtue are not matters of fact to be exposed by reason, but feelings with no more authority than that they happen to us. Even murder turns out to be nothing but an event toward which one has a possibly unreasonable feeling of dislike. Hume is specific on the point, with all the blandness of a man who does not expect to be murdered. In his view murder is no more and no less than any other death. De Sade thought the same. However, certain acts, no matter how we describe them, have aroused not tepid feelings of dislike, but passions of rage and horror down the ages which have even exploded society into revolution. The unjust condemnation of Dreyfus is an example. Oppressive property rights, tyrannical government, bad laws, slavery, denial of nationhood, racialism, are among them. So too is incest which in the Theban legend felled a king. The impact of classical Greece (and so, in one sense, of primitive society) has perhaps been greatest in our century in the story of Oedipus. It is central to the whole doctrine of Freud, who uses it anthropologically to describe the genesis of civilization and morals, and psychologically to explain the emergence, out of infancy, of the disciplined and structured human mind. The Freudian doctrine, in fact, pronounces on the significance of the discovery of incest for human moral birth. We note however that for the people of Thebes it was not the subjective feelings of Oedipus which were a guide to their judgment. They understood his innocence and mourned his fall. But ignorance was no acquittal, it was the objective facts of parricide and incest which condemned him. They constituted not simply a disturbance of the civilized order but of the natural order too. The same horror of "objective fact" is present in the Balinese attitude to twins of opposing sexes. Their intra-uterine cohabitation is seen as an incestuous union of brother and sister, even though it occurs before the birth of consciousness.

Freud did not overestimate the significance of the discovery of incest. Sacred exceptions apart,[2] it is not difficult to conclude that dread of incest is universal. It does not matter what primitive people one examines, incest meets with the severest condemnation and is held to merit exile or death. It provokes an emotional shock far greater than murder arouses, the participants are conceived to be changed by this deed and in an irreversible sense so that nothing they subsequently do can restore the pre-incestuous status to them: they are dehumanized, detribalized.

Margaret Mead, in *Coming of Age in Samoa,* explained that relatives of opposite sex "have a most rigid code of etiquette prescribed for all their contacts. After they have reached the age of discretion —nine or ten years of age in this case—they may not touch each other, sit close to each other, eat together, address each other familiarly, or mention any salacious matter in each other's presence." [3] The list of taboos grows inordinately. They can't remain in a house together, unless in a crowd. They can't walk together, dance on the same floor, take part in common activities or even use each other's property—and this total separation which applies "to all individuals of the opposite sex within five years above or below one's own age or to whom one acknowledges any relationship by blood or marriage," [4] begins in childhood and comes to an end only in toothless old age. Even, she explains, if an older man falls in love with some young and dependent woman or girl of his household, his adopted child or wife's younger sister for example, the accusation of incest, even in the absence of the deed, is raised against him and the feeling of the village may run so high that he is forced to leave the group.

Bronislaw Malinowski, in his classic *The Sexual Life of Savages,* has parallel accounts of the Trobrianders, those attractive pagans whose life he watched with such minute and loving care. When a Trobriand boy grows up, and there is a sister of his living in his hut, he has to go and sleep in the bachelors' house. It is not really a house reserved exclusively to youths, as in some primitive societies, but a place where young men carry on undisturbed their liaisons with the concubines they take before marriage. The dismissal of nubile youths to the bachelors' club has nothing to do with the preservation of sexual morality in general, but is a consequence of the etiquette which forbids him to live under the same roof as his sister. Even accidental contact between brother and sister is eliminated in this way.

In her own love affairs the sister is under strict necessity to avoid being seen by her brother. The Trobrianders told Malinowski that if by chance a man discovered his sister while she was making love to her sweetheart, disgrace would fall on all three, and all three would have to commit suicide by jumping from a coconut palm in obedience to the prescribed manner of public atonement. "When, on certain occasions, brother and sister have to appear in the same company—when they travel in the same canoe, for instance, or participate in a domestic meeting—a rigidity of behavior and a sobriety of conversation fall upon all those present. No cheerful company, no festive entertainment, therefore, is allowed to include brother and sister, since their simultaneous presence would throw a blight on pleasure and would chill gaiety." [5]

The punishment Trobriand society demands for incest is suicide. But so sharp and anguished is the public consciousness of the disgrace of incest that even the public but unproved accusation of incest was, Malinowski was told, so mortal a blow to a person's honor that suicide followed as a matter of course. "What would happen," the skeptical Malinowski asked, "if incest were not discovered?" He was given the answer that it produced a painful and probably fatal disease. The belly swells, the skin becomes white and breaks out into sores and the criminal "fades away in a wasting sickness."

It is important however to realize what is meant by "brother" and "sister" in the Trobriand context, or the Western connotations will deceive us. The Trobriand word *luguta* is applied by a man to his sister or a woman to her brother; but it is also applied by a man to a woman of the same clan and generation and vice versa, that is to say to all of one generation who are taboo to each other and therefore stand technically in the brother-sister relationship. The incest taboo of course is wider than this relationship—it covers parents and one's own children of the opposite sex and the tender word *lubaygu* can never be applied to the *ludaytasi*—that is to the women of the same clan. This is an extremely good example of the value of a social institution in the prevention even of accidental incest. By the rejection of *any* legal endogamous sexual relation-ships—any relationship at all with members of one's own clan—long absence, the death of parents, the uprooting of homes, which might produce the cessation of contact or the loss of knowledge of kinship relations or any other accidents which might have opened the door to incest, are avoided. A Trobriand Oedipus could never have married his mother if once he had been made aware of his clan membership, and she of hers, no matter how great the separa-tion of time and place. Nevertheless, it does appear that these pre-cautions were over-elaborate. Though "incest with the own sister is . . . a dreadful crime to the natives," incest with members of the clan not in genealogical relation did take place and was sometimes boasted about, even though socially and morally disapproved. But the fact even of overprovision is important too in a primitive society whose members do not associate sexual intercourse with childbear-ing (or swear they do not, at least). It suggests a profound if un-conscious understanding of what is involved in sex—that its ex-plosive power in society would hardly be less even if it had no direct relationship to the bearing of children.

Malinowski relates a tragic myth of incest as evidence of the imaginative power and appeal of incest to the minds of the primi-tive islanders. It concerns two beautiful children, brother and sister. The boy had collected magical herbs and cooked them in coconut oil to make a love potion. He hung the vessel containing the love fluid from the roof near the door of the family hut. There he left it and went away to bathe in the lagoon. His sister returned from gathering firewood and presently entered the hut. Her head brushed against the bottle containing the magic potion, it trickled into her hair, she passed her hands over her head and wiped off the oil and smelled it and the magic entered into her. Trembling, she asked where her brother had gone and her mother said, "O my children have gone mad! He has gone to the seashore." The girl ran toward the open sea. When she came to the beach she untied her fiber skirt and threw it away. She ran naked along the beach, seeking her brother, and found him bathing. She entered the water and gave chase to him up and down the lagoon and finally caught him and they lay down together in the warm sea and had intercourse with each other. Overcome with passion they went together to the grotto on the seashore, a local landmark, and there they lay together again and again but did not eat or drink, for they were filled with shame. And so they died, unparted. A fisherman of Iwa had a dream that same night. He dreamed of the mint plant which is used to make love potions and that two people, brother and sister, were lying together in the island grotto through its power. He went out that day and searched for them and as he climbed the slope toward the grotto a frigate bird rose, as though it had caught the scent of humans. The bird's flight led him toward them and soon he caught sight of the prostrate figures and lo! a mint flower had sprouted through their breasts.

There is a tenderness in the telling of the story and this reflects the delicacy with which the Trobrianders handle their sexual problems. Malinowski speaks of the native contempt for exhibitionism and for too insistent and ungallant pursuit of woman. They despise the lack of success in lovemaking which this points to. Their whole attitude to excess, he explains, displays "an appreciation of restraint and dignity . . . the moral command not to violate, solicit, or touch is founded on a strong conviction that it is shameful; and shameful because real worth lies in being coveted, in conquering by charm, by beauty and by magic." All the threads of his account weave into one complex pattern of manners, morals and aesthetic taste, he explains.

All in all, in Malinowski's study, we see at work the irresistible will to "make over" sex in a social way, to impose upon it patterns and permissions which are in accord with the tribal pride. Even the aesthetic judgments are ways of saying what is allowable humanly speaking and what is not. What this evidence reveals to us is the socializing or the civilizing of sex. Sex is placed under other disciplines than the biological, and all that might endanger the social life is brought under ferocious condemnation.

2

It may not be so, of course, but it often looks as though the horror of incest was the fundamental moral aversion, the fundamental moral decision of humanity, and we may assert this not only through the insights of Freud but by the evidence of anthropology. In *Nature Into History* where I first posed this, I asked *why?*—and came to the conclusion that incest was the sin against all because its primary threat was against the very existence of society itself. In the examples we have seen the most damaging form of incest, that most legislated against in primitive societies, is brother-sister incest. It springs from the strong possibility of sexual attraction between nubile children in constant contact, which law can forbid but cannot prevent. If not proscribed it can lead to a lifelong incestuous union which could be endlessly repeated—parental incest leading to incest with offspring and incest among the offspring, to the family itself as the bitter center of sexual rivalries and conquests. Such a conflict would be the negation even of the *biological* role of the family in protecting the offspring from all aggression and nurturing the young toward maturity and independence. But society too, not only the family, is threatened by incest. If a family cannot protect its members against themselves how can it resist the depredations of others? And if it fails, then it could be tit for tat, the contagion spreading, and a basis for both family and society vanishing. A promiscuous, murdering horde might be left in which men would live, in Thomas Hobbes' words, in "continual fear, and danger of violent death; and the life of man, solitary, poor, nasty, brutish and short." Such hordes may have existed and vanished like grass. Probably we shall never know. But those societies which did succeed in controlling their strongest and potentially most antisocial passions and in turning their aggression away from sexual objects would have the highest survival value and be more likely to create cultures which would be remembered. That seems a reasonable hypothesis.

Deeper reasons can be sought. Legislation against brother-sister incest comes not from children themselves, but from society. The elders can see what children in their innocence cannot see. A rigid tribal etiquette forbidding any sort of intimacy between the tiniest of brothers and sisters and making the brother the punctilious guardian of manners and morals when the sister is present is a means of compelling the children to learn the meaning of incest. Malinowski says, for instance, that the Trobriand child is seldom punished or even scolded and so receives a real shock when it is roughly handled and loudly reprimanded for some "friendly, affectionate, or even playful advances to the other small being constantly about in the same household." He speaks of an "emotional contagion" born out of the perception of the moral reactions of others.

The *primary* incestuous opportunity, the first temptation, is that which is presented to parents by the accessibility of their own young. And against this no possible social institution can erect a barrier. Nothing can, and nothing ought to separate parents psychologically or physically from their children. Nor of course could a family function if parents could not handle and fondle, feed and clean and correct the bodies of their children. The close physical intimacy which follows birth is an extension of the intra-uterine union of the child with the mother and is itself a beautiful and humanizing relation. The offspring of most warm-blooded creatures enjoy a special relationship of dependence, tenderness and confidence with their parents, and particularly with the mother. So completely realized is this family relationship at the human level that the relationship created by a birth is one which endures, accidents apart, for the lifetimes both of the children and the parents. It is not extinguished by maturity or by death.

Conventions strictly govern brother-sister relations in many primitive societies. Conventions also play a role in the parent-child relation. Social approval governs punishments and rewards and the language and attitudes of parents to children and children to parents. But the ultimate barrier to incestuous relations between parents and their young is not a conventional but a moral one and this arises precisely because human beings are endowed with hindsight and foresight. I think that what was discovered in the first human societies was the choice between incest and love.

The love which exists between parents and children is not of the order of sexual love and it is recognized by all, no matter what the status of the society to which they belong, as capable of being destroyed by lust. If the parent knows this out of experience, and at the same time foresees the future through which the child must be guided and helped, he (or she) must understand too that if he pursues the satisfaction of lust through his own offspring, he must by the act of incest, directed to the children, risk destroying that delicate relationship which is a source of inner spiritual stature as well as of social standing. The possession of upright, innocent sons, of beautiful virgin daughters, has been, down the ages, a source of fierce pride. In fact, incest is an act of self- and family-destruction. If, notwithstanding, the satisfaction of lust is embarked upon at the expense of the offspring, the parent must now turn one or more of his children into the object of temporary and probably secret intercourse, or "espouse" it openly and so break with the legitimate partner, rousing in the process a hatred and jealousy which would make insecure the lives of both offenders, and render the task of caring for the rest of the family very hard. The family would dissolve, only the promiscuous sexual horde might conceivably take its place. Moreover the parent would have to face a future bereft of all those continuing elements of family and kinship which are even more important to primitive people than to civilized ones.

It is not simply that the element of love and tenderness would make doubly horrible the act of lust; that alone might be overborne. But man's mind works backward and forward along the dimension of time, seeing what has been and what might be, and, before ever evil is committed, seeing all that might flow from one act of his loins.

There is a sense in which an animal or a bird lives only in the present. The animal cycle of bird life is not something the bird appears to plan or even to anticipate. It moves from one inborn response to another and knows nothing of its birth or death, at least at the level of consciousness. Man, however, is never just what he is at one moment of time. He is a being who has a structure in time, able to recall the past in memory and to evoke the future in imagination, anticipating his own needs and the dangers and opportunities of the future, and making provision in advance to ward off the one and to exploit the other. It is the discovery of the degree of his own responsibility and freedom of maneuver along the dimension of time which makes man a moral being. The discovery is never a solitary one but is always within a social nexus. Not only does the growing child discover his own history, but he discovers his genealogy, his nexus of kin stretching its filaments everywhere in a larger society, and finally he discovers that larger society with an existence and power of its own and a history which explains and sustains his own personal and familial existence.

Man therefore is this historical being, through and through. The living of this historical being demands that he shall seek to enter into the lives of others as imaginatively as he enters into his own. There is something remarkable, and essentially unnatural, in the ability man possesses to put himself sympathetically in the minds of others, but then too, David Hume might say, there is something remarkable and unnatural in the condemnation of incest. The two are linked in man's inward discovery of his sympathetic and imaginative self and of his responsibility for his acts. The discovery of incest is man's first great moral leap, perhaps the moral leap by which he becomes man, for through it man realizes that he is no longer as the animals and can never become as the animals again without abandoning his treasured human condition. The establishment of a discipline over sexual activity would seem to be the first condition for the birth of human society. This is a process we might better understand by examining the relationship between the struggle for tribal identity and the rite of circumcision.

CHAPTER four

SEX AS THE
GIFT OF SOCIETY

1

Today, it is often argued, mankind is moving toward uniformity—the same kind of dress, the same mass-produced commodities, the same buildings, towns, traffic jams and brutal architecture, the same scientific culture the world over. If true, it is a new phenomenon. In the past cultures moved away from each other and so distinct were they that Spengler could not imagine their cross-fertilization. Certainly no tribe has ever seemed content with its own biological birthright. At whatever point the anthropologist cuts into the tribal life he discovers this cultural dimension in which the tribe has its being. It amounts to a distinct style which reflects itself in huts or houses, in pottery and household goods, in weapons and canoes, in clothes and decorations. It expresses itself in woad or paint, in feathered headdresses or clay-fortified hair, in armbands, necklaces, girdles, pubic coverings and the other endless contrivances for the better display or concealment of human bodies. It is reflected in the body itself, in cosmetic activities such as depilation, shaving, hairdressing, oiling of the skin, or physical mutilation such as tattooing, scarification, amputation, circumcision. It is the very essence of language, song, dance, ritual, ceremony, convention, and the processes and content of education and government. It has its birth in and weaves itself around the economic activities of society and the biological dimensions which define and confine man—procreation, birth, death. It heightens the human drama and proclaims the tribal or national identity, separating the people from other groups and from nature itself.

Although anthropologists properly relate tribal culture to the economic basis of the tribe, to the means of livelihood, to the scope provided by the environment, the point is these bases set limits to what can be done rather than tell how the politico-cultural life comes into being. As a matter of fact, seventeenth- and eighteenth-century thinkers found it inconceivable that the most primitive state of mankind was anything else but a state of complete individual independence. For Hobbes and Locke and Rousseau, man in a state of nature was free and sovereign. He was under no man's rule, and subject to no tribe's tyranny. And the atomization of primitive mankind in this way was to them such an inescapable human birthright that the real difficulty was to show why man ever surrendered his animal freedom and gave to society that dangerous sovereignty over his life and liberty, his private gift from God, which society anyway so often and so openly abused. These thinkers disagreed as to the nature of the inducements which caused man to surrender his liberty, but they were at one in describing society as an artificial contrivance of man, and not as the given basis of man's humanity.

Sigmund Freud saw this problem and discussed it in *Totem and Taboo,* inevitably in a sexual context. In most animal societies, gregariousness is greatest during periods of sexual quiescence. Perhaps the flocking of birds in the autumn and winter is the best example of this. Once the herd or flock wakens from its sexual sleep, then some atomization of the flock takes place. The bird flocks of many species entirely disappear and in their place we find the multitude of bird pairs whose loyalty is only to their nest and broods and who are at enmity with other pairs. The sexual urges are too great to permit the tolerance necessary to keep the flock in existence; the flock itself is possibly also the economic enemy of the family group. But with man there is no close sexual season—no time therefore when gregariousness is less dangerous or explosive than others. And Freud saw that if society with all its prohibitions, disciplines and taboos, many of them strongly sexual, had come into existence against, so to speak, the powerful but anarchic sexual urges of the young male, then there had really to be a unique explanation for an event so contrary to nature. And Freud knew of no urge greater than the sexual urge, and he could not justify so remarkable a repression of man's sexuality at the behest of society except in terms of the explanation habitual to him, that the same energy which was the source of man's sexual drive could be turned into a sexual brake.

To Freud's argument I shall recur. But what I have so far said must have made it clear that—if we except the insects which have been physiologically adapted to the servile life of the insect state —no animal in a wild state is prepared to submit voluntarily to the will of another, or to endure any limitations to the exercise of its natural powers and functions save those which necessity or the pecking order imposes. If there is food, it will eat; if not, it cannot. If food is available, or if a mate is available, and anything seeks to restrain it, it will struggle to assert itself, and run away if defeated. Man alone chooses another way. Only man, while establishing control over natural things, unnaturally surrenders rights over his life and liberties to the society into which he is born.

As to how this potentially sovereign natural being is able to turn upon the nature with which he is endowed and subdue it or crush it is, as the social contract theorists saw, indeed an enigma. I may be excused from seeking to unravel it at this point, I think; but if it is uncertain how it is done, we do know precisely *what* has to be done. It is what Hobbes tells us about in *Leviathan*. Man has to give his allegiance to something other than his natural gifts and impulses. He must step outside nature into another frame of reference, a frame which in contrast with nature is going to be artificial —for this other frame is not a birthright, but in a sense is at first completely unknown, and grasped at with difficulty and constructed and maintained with infinite pain and endless labor. It is the ledge above aboriginal man of which Toynbee spoke in a vivid passage [1] which man struggles to reach, and when he reaches it, its vantage point enables him to see things below him in another perspective and to recognize *the separation which has taken place and which has lifted him out of nature,* a separation he seeks by all means in his power to perpetuate.

It is certainly true that no known tribe is satisfied simply with that distinction which its private pattern of genes awards it. The natural tribal physique is not enough, and every human group seeks its own style to enhance or transform its original endowments. If we look first at some circumcision rites and what they involve we may better understand the intention of these activities.

2

In one of their monumental tomes, Spencer and Gillen discuss the initiation rites of the northern tribes of Central Australia for boys at or approaching puberty.[2] These are not the only initiation ceremonies of these tribes. Some of the coastal tribes practice the knocking out of one or more of the upper incisor teeth. They speak too of a tribe, the Lakaria, in the country near Port Darwin, which practiced yet another form of initiation. The youths who had arrived at the age of puberty were taken away and isolated by the old men of the tribe, and subject to rude buffets and tests. Blows were aimed at them, or food kept from them, or they were set to climb or fell large trees, or to swim in crocodile-infested rivers, and to endure these humiliations and dangers without grumbling. Only at the end, when this initiation was safely accomplished, were the youths shown the tribal bull-roarer, whose voice women believed to be that of a spirit which came down from the sky, and then taken away into the bush from which they were to return initiated men. And even the most painful and cruel initiations practiced by these savages maintained a similar element of sacredness.

In the Urunna tribe, we are told, when the time has come for the boy's initiation, his paternal grandfather seizes hold of him and after some ceremonies before the women which are meant to mark him as an initiate, the boy goes upon a journey with his mentor, rather like a *chela* with his *guru,* visiting different groups and inviting them to the ceremony. Upon this journey the persons of the boy and his guardian are sacred and may not be attacked by fellow tribesmen. Upon their return there follow several nights of ceremonies before the boy is finally circumcised by the elderly male relatives tradition assigns to the task. He is taken away into the bush and kept incommunicado until he has recovered, and then brought back and immediately, with as much ceremony, subincised. When this is over, he is shown, on the same night, more sacred totemic ceremonies, and the elderly male relatives who have supervised the initiation tell him that he is now a man and not a boy. He must not attempt intercourse with *lubras* other than his lawful wives, and he is not on any account to interfere with the *lubras* belonging to other men. If he breaks the taboos he will fall down dead like the stones. Only after all this may he sit in the men's camp, and take a wife to himself.

A deeply sympathetic observer of the aborigine, Charles P. Mountford, describes the ceremony of tribal expulsion in this vivid fashion:

One evening . . . the happy, carefree life of one of their number is completely shattered. Closely related women, his source of comfort in every childish trouble, suddenly attack him, and, with blazing firesticks, drive him from the camp. By that ceremonial expulsion the lad is deprived of the affection and indulgence of the women, and forced to live under the dominance of the gruff, unresponsive old men, his tutors on the long difficult road to tribal manhood. From then, until the circumcision ceremonies are completed, perhaps in a year or so, the youth is treated as an outcast. He always sleeps at some distance from the main camp; never goes near or calls out to the women; nor does he speak to the old men unless first addressed, and then his reply must not be above a whisper. It is a most drastic break, and the youth must be thoroughly puzzled and distressed over the many prohibitions that have so quickly surrounded him. . . . Eventually the day comes when he is pounced upon by the old men, and, to the accompaniment of the wailing of the women and the shouting and stamping of the already initiated men, he is led to the secret grounds.

During the initiation rituals the men who stand in close relationship to him open the veins in their arms and allow the blood to pour over his body. The fundamental idea behind this custom is that blood is *kuranita* (life essence), and the giving of ample supplies of blood will provide the initiate with the necessary health and vitality to grow to strong and virile manhood.[3]

The ceremonies of some tribes are of infinite complication, but in the main what is common to them all is that the boy is taken away from the women's camp in a ceremonial fashion which marks the end of his childhood, he is shown to those tribal groups which should attend the ceremony, he is brought back to sacred grounds normally taboo to women, and there ceremonies are endlessly performed within his hearing though not always within his sight. The dances and ceremonial plays and displays may go on for several days, before the dazed child is circumcised. The moment when this will occur is normally hidden from him, and he cannot know what to expect, save that he may be put to death and brought to life again by the tribal or totemic spirit, as the women will have warned him. The initiation may include mock attacks on him with spears; but as no initiate ever reveals to those younger what he passes through, he does not know that one of those spears will not presently pierce him. When the ceremony is over, and only then, his sacred totem or totem sign will be revealed to him, and it is made known that he is now a man and can sit with the men and take a wife. The awfulness of the ceremonies is increased by the magical use of blood, in the manner Charles P. Mountford has pointed out; but then blood from the boy's own wounds may also be used ritually—it may be given to the mother and father to drink, or sucked by the youth from the knife which cut him, or smeared on the backs of the officiating old men. In many tribes it is regarded as dreadful for the blood to be allowed to fall to the ground.

Spencer and Gillen said of the initiation ceremonies: "We tried in vain to find any satisfactory explanation of the ceremonies of circumcision and subincision, but so far as we could discover the native has no idea whatever of what these ceremonies mean . . . it is rather a curious fact that they have not invented some tradition to explain their meaning." [4] However, John Layard, in *The Stone*

Men of Malekula: Vao, describing the elaborate ceremonies of the New Hebrides, said that the mutilation or removal of the foreskin represented a departure from nature which was "liable to call down the wrath of nature. In its cultural aspect it is a sign of manhood and of man's ability, through sacrifice, to conquer nature, expressed in the phrase that till a youth is incised he is 'only a woman.' " [5]

The best evidence of the purpose of circumcision in the eyes of tribal peoples of all kinds is the passage in Genesis, where the Lord declares: "This is my covenant, which ye shall keep, between me and you and thy seed after thee; every male among you shall be circumcised. And ye shall be circumcised in the flesh of your foreskin; and it shall be a token of a covenant betwixt me and you. And he that is eight days old shall be circumcised among you, every male throughout your generations, he that is born in thy house, or bought with money of any stranger, which is not of thy seed. He that is born in thy house, and he that is bought with thy money, must needs be circumcised; and my covenant shall be in your flesh for an everlasting covenant. And the uncircumcised male who is not circumcised in the flesh of his foreskin, that soul shall be cut off from his people; he hath broken my covenant." [6]

The Jews were the most profoundly religious people the world has ever seen, and it was impossible for them to conceive of circumcision outside their relationship with God. And so in that proud statement, pregnant with remorseless purpose, circumcision is declared the seal of God in the flesh of man. Those who have it not shall be cast out. There could hardly be a more remarkable example of circumcision as a badge of tribal identity. And because for the Jews it is a badge, not a personal initiation, it is important to perform it in infancy rather than at puberty when its significance might be confused by its association with the emergence of sexual powers. It is not the only badge we can find. Among some African tribes the last joint of the little finger is chopped off. Cave drawings in France show Stone Age men with precisely the same mutilation. The Maoris tattooed their bodies in intricate and beautiful patterns. The Nuer peoples of the Nile cut a deep scar across the forehead of the young initiates; marks of it are found even upon the skulls of the dead. The Piorias of the Orinoco dope the initiates with drink and drugs and over their bodies pass webs of fierce stinging ants, then beat the children in the village square. Many African tribes practice scarification, again in elaborate patterns of aesthetic and social significance. The Eskimos file their teeth, to make them less like those of dogs. The piercing of the septum, the wearing of nose rings and earrings, the deformation of the skull or of the bones of the neck or of the genital organs—there is almost no end to the deliberate and distinctive mutilations or decorations of the body associated with tribal recognition. And in very many cases these other mutilations are practiced side by side with circumcision, cliterodectomy, and subincision.

It is the remarkable popularity of circumcision among primitive peoples that compels one to ask whether it has greater significance than simply to act as a badge of tribal recognition, and the hoary antiquity of the practice was perhaps revealed unconsciously by Spencer and Gillen when they said that the natives could not account for it, and had not even invented a myth or story to justify it. That seems to make it as much a matter of course to them as the air they breathed, so much taken for granted as part of the tribal order that explanation was considered unnecessary. Of course, there have been other explanations. One is that circumcision masks the castration threat. Sigmund Freud has associated circumcision with anti-Semitism, seeking to explain that people unconsciously become anti-Semitic because circumcision is associated in their minds with the threat against male virility. The argument generally, I suppose, is that youth at puberty becomes the rival of the old males of the tribe, and circumcision is simply what is left of the threat (or perhaps practice) of castration of the sexually anarchic young males. In that case circumcision is simply a substitute for castration as animal sacrifice is sometimes a substitute for human sacrifice.

This is at once too simple and too sophisticated an explanation. It overlooks first that the dominant tribal element, even in those aboriginal tribes we have been considering, consists of the *old* men, jealous guardians of the tribal mores and tribal existence. They, the sexually spent, would have been less deeply affected by sexual rivalry of the boys than would be the young tribal bulls in their prime. It is a necessary part of the tribal system that the old males should triumph politically and socially over the young males of the tribes, as well as over the impotent children. The youth at puberty is less able, sexually and economically, to challenge the old men of the tribe than is the male in his prime. It is against the male in his prime, if against anyone, that the old male would have been justified in launching his castration threat. And then too, why castration? Why not, simply, murder? Primitive peoples do not shrink from murder, and murder would have been simpler and more successful than leaving a useless and conceivably revengeful tribal eunuch to sour the tribal life. But there is no evidence at all of the practice of castration in primitive tribes, except of dead or dying male enemies as a sign of triumph. And I think, too, that anthropologists have disposed of the idea that circumcision and subincision have any relation to a wish to restrict population by some kind of birth control. It is a remedy which would never occur, in any case, to primitive people who do not associate sexual intercourse with pregnancy, or who, if they do, yet believe that the entry of the ancestral spirit into the womb of the mother is at least as essential an element in conception as copulation, and may occur independently of the sexual act. Such views may have been more widespread among primitive peoples than they are now. Besides, as Spencer and Gillen say, what simpler remedy to hand than infanticide, which is still practiced and was known throughout antiquity?

Among primitive peoples, where circumcision is practiced at or near puberty, it is certainly not regarded as a punishment, but as a sign of virility, and of acceptance into the tribal maleness. It is the uncircumcised boy who is jeered at as a woman, and made the object of general mockery. In African tribes it is the uncircumcised one who is the irresponsible one, free to break tribal taboos, defiance of which would strike his elders down dead. Indeed, the act of circumcision is the entry into, not the threat of deprival of, male sexual privileges. In *The Origins and History of Consciousness* Erich Neumann writes that the initiations and "the trials of endurance are tests of the virility and stability of the ego; they are not to be taken personalistically as 'the vengeance of the old' upon the young, any more than our matriculation is the vengeance of old men upon the rising generation, but merely a certificate of maturity for entry into the collective. In almost all cases, age brings an increase in power and importance based on the increased knowledge gained through successive initiations, so that the old men have little case for resentment." [7] Neumann links the specifically male initiations not with sexual or genital roles at all, but with the rise of the *assertive male consciousness*. They are the mark of its liberation from the matriarchate. Male self-assertion, so manifest in those male initiations from which women are excluded on pain of death, and which may not even be reported to them, is a witness to the birth of higher consciousness in man, of an intellectual and managerial capacity which deliberately cuts itself off from the intuitive and generally blurring female consciousness, a male power only capable of coming to birth when the tie with the female consciousness is broken. "The higher masculinity here in point has no phallic or chthonic accent; its content is not, as in many initiations of young girls, sexuality, but its counterpole, spirit, which appears together with light, the sun, the head, and the eye as symbols of consciousness. This spirit is what is accentuated, and into it the initiations lead." [8]

I accept in general this argument. However, for entry into the male circle or the tribal collective any systematic initiation would serve, and obviously does serve, for we know not all initiations involve circumcision, and many are performed on what is sometimes spoken of as man's secondary or higher sexuality—his head. Nevertheless the universality of circumcision and its relation to the genitalia makes it specially significant, for the more widespread its use the less effective it is as a badge of recognition whether in the scriptural or the tribal sense. It must then be significant in other ways. And here one may venture one or two observations.

Circumcision is generally, though not always, performed around puberty. It has therefore a very special sexual pointing. It is a painful operation, associated with the advent of sexual powers, *but imposed by the tribe*. What must it serve to do in the child's mind? First, to make him feel that his sexual maturity is, in a sense, within the gift of the tribe; then, to deepen the awe and mystery which

surround the generative powers; then, by the pain and misery tem-
porarily inflicted upon him, to breed in him the consciousness that
the tribe stands over the sexual powers, able by pain to subdue
pleasure whenever it needs to. And this complex of ideas, made
more vivid by the ceremonies themselves, marks the entry of the
boy into the sphere of strict sexual taboos and marital and economic and political responsibilities, where sex can be no longer
wholly play, indeed into the sphere where all its manifestations *at
last* carry social consequences.

Of course, puberty is itself a physical transformation of a total
kind. It produces a new being, and the passage through puberty
brings with it the sense of being born into a new world and the
"death" of the child and the "birth" of the man is an important
part of all pubertal *rites de passage*. In the Poro Society of Liberia
a most elaborate form of deception used to be practiced. At the
entrance to the ceremonial camp in which their circumcision and
subsequent scarification would take place, and in which they would
remain for three years, a ceremonial "death" of the youths took
place. "In the old days they [the boys] were apparently run through
with a spear and tossed over the curtain. Onlookers heard a thud
as he [the boy] was supposed to hit the ground inside, dead. Actually, the boy was protected by a chunk of plantain stalk tied on
under his clothes. Into this the spear was thrust. A bladder of
chicken's blood at the right spot was punctured and spilled to make
it all very realistic to other boys and women who could not resist
the desire to see their sons for the last time. Inside the fence the
officer and two assistants, all masked, caught the boys in mid-air,
and dropped a heavy dummy to complete the delusion. The boys
were actually unharmed, and were quickly carried away into the
deep forest which is the Poro grove." [9] Even the subsequent painful scarifying ceremonies had a death and rebirth theme. The scars
were supposed to be the marks of the great crocodile spirit which
had swallowed the boys and in whose belly they had lived during
their stay in the bush. Initiation here becomes pure melodrama,
almost slapstick.

3

We have to recognize that all these ceremonies of initiation encounter a psychological resistance. The more painful they are, the greater the reluctance of the initiates to face them, and the greater the suffering of the parents and other adults at the pain they have to inflict. All such acts of mutilation have to take place against emotional shrinking; indeed much of their value arises out of the general resistance which has to be overcome. We cannot understand these things if we forget what it is to be human. When we are faced with unpleasant duties we tend to postpone them, or to find reasons for not doing them, or simply fail to remember them. This lazy postponement or actual forgetting must always have faced man in his tribal condition too. It is therefore important to realize that the ritual heightening of the ceremonies of initiation has precisely the intention of making the whole event tribally memorable and spiritually significant and irresistible. Long prepatory rites and ceremonies and elaborate dances produce exaltation in initiates and participants alike. They launch the whole tribe or village or clan into a spiritual glissade which gathers momentum, and of which the climax is the painful mutilation of the young. And once launched upon the ceremonial cycle, it presently becomes inconceivable that the whole drama should not mount to its great climax. Even the initiates become as sleepwalkers, carried on irresistibly by the great drama. In *The Dark Child* Camara Laye, a young Negro from French Guinea, has written what must be the first account of what it means to be a tribal initiate, in a book which is a minor literary masterpiece.

It was not without misgivings that I approached this transition from childhood to manhood; the thought of it really caused me great distress, as it did those who were to share the ordeal. . . . But however great the anxiety, however certain the pain, no one would have dreamed of running away from the ordeal—no more than one would have dreamed of running away from the ordeal of the lions—and I for my own part never entertained such thoughts. I wanted to be born, to be born again. I knew perfectly well that I was going to be hurt, but I wanted to be a man and it seemed to me that nothing could be too painful if, by enduring it, I was to come to man's estate. My companions felt the same; like myself, they were prepared to pay for it with their blood. Our elders before us had paid for it thus; those who were born after us would pay for it in their turn. Why should we be spared? Life itself would spring from the shedding of our blood.[10]

There were two aspects of the ceremony, the public rejoicing and the secret initiation. In the public ceremony, the whole village was given over to noisy festival. For a whole week Camara and his companions, already lodged in a special enclosure, danced in the main square day after day the dance of those who are to be circumcised. "Were we not dancing to forget what we were all dreading?" The whole town danced with them. "In our country, all dances have this cumulative tendency, because each beat of the tom-tom has an almost irresistible appeal." [11] Men, women and girls outdid the youths in frenzy. And then, after days of endless and exhausting dances, the specially clothed initiates were taken into the bush, into a sacred place. The old and famous "operator" appeared with his knives, and in a few seconds, Camara Laye relates, the dozen or so boys "became men." The boys were shocked by the abundant flow of blood; only when it had more or less ceased could their wounds be dressed.

"When the blood had finally ceased flowing, we were dressed in our long boubou again. Apart from a very brief undershirt, this was to be our only article of attire during the weeks of convalescence that were to come. We stood up awkwardly, light-headed and sick at our stomachs. Among the men who had been present at the operation, I saw several who, taking pity on our plight, turned their heads away to hide their tears." [12] The boys returned to the feast in their honor, the social climax of the affair, but could not eat, for all had a touch of fever. Perhaps for days, in their strict seclusion, under ceaseless watch and nursing at the hands of special male attendants, they would have this fever. Not until three weeks had passed could Camara see his mother, nor until after four weeks was he allowed any liberty. The circumcised boys were obviously ritually taboo; but they were also medically isolated in order to speed up their recovery, for what indeed was inflicted upon them was much the same as a serious illness.

Some teaching accompanied the rite. The boys were commanded to be honest, to fulfill their duties toward God, and toward their parents and superiors, and to befriend their neighbors. There was nothing, the young man relates, not fit for other ears than their own. The moral tone was appropriate to a Christian Sunday school; and indeed it seems that this would also be true of the secret ethical instructions given to aboriginal initiates in Australia. Merely to impart such ethical instruction, so awesome and painful a ceremony was hardly necessary. No, the principal part of the ceremony was "becoming men." But the boys would have become men in the course of nature anyway, and so the passage into manhood marked by the ceremony was either gratuitous or else was much more than a guarantee of that which nature had in any case given them. The clue to the meaning of the ceremony is in the declaration which Camara makes of solidarity with the tribe—that he will be like them, and pass through the same ordeals, and pay for his tribal identity with his blood. It is, in fact, not the entry into manhood as such which the ceremony marks, but the entry into the realm where mere manhood or mere maturity has to be subordinated even through suffering to the demands of the tribe. That is to say it is not his natural but his social, or political, person which was born. But that social and political person inherits a responsibility for a minutely structured society. In short, it is a *spiritual* inheritance into which the boy is born, an inheritance which from the very beginning carries its burden of pain and suffering, though these are not always of a physical nature.

There is, in one tribal history, an interesting association of circumcision with technical advances. It is told by Spencer and Gillen in a legend of the Kaitish aborigines:

In the Alcheringa two eggs were laid in a nest at Unjuia, out of which came two Ullakuppera (little hawk) boys. The elder one broke through the shell first, and when he had come out he listened and heard the younger brother making a noise in his shell, so he broke it and set him free. The younger one coming out said, "Hullo, where is my father?" and the elder one said, "We have no father or mother."

The younger one said, "Which way shall we walk, shall we go towards the Altimala (west)?" but the elder one merely stood up and said nothing. Then the younger one said, "Shall we walk towards the Okniroka (east)?" but the elder one did not reply for some time, and at last said, "We will walk to the Altranga (north)." Then they set off. As they went along they gradually increased in size until, when they reached a hill a little to the north of the Foster Range, called Karrarinia, their pubic hairs were beginning to appear. All along the way they met with incomplete human beings called *inter-intera*, who, like the two boys, were continually trying to pull their foreskins back. Up in the sky there dwelt a great being called Atnatu, who had a black face and no *atna* (anus). Looking down he saw the two boys walking about searching for rats, and pulling their foreskins back in the hope of making themselves into young men. They went out on three or four successive days, and on the fifth the elder boy went out alone amongst the hills. To his surprise he saw what at first he thought was a big leaf tumbling down, but on catching it in his hands he found that it was a large *leilirra*—a stone knife—sent down by Atnatu. He at once circumcised himself with it and then returned to camp, where his younger brother on seeing him said, "Hullo, my big brother has been and cut himself." Then the younger brother went out into the bush, and once more Atnatu sent down a knife with which the boy cut himself and returned to camp, where the elder brother saw what had happened and said, "Hullo, my little brother has been and cut himself." Then the two sat down opposite each other and performed the rite of subincision, and the blood of the elder boy flowed right away across the Barrow Creek flats, carving out a creek bed which still remains. It flowed on until it reached Urkampitjera, a spot some twenty miles away to the north. The blood of the younger boy flowed to the north-west, and made a little creek running down from the Foster Range to the north; then it went on to Kopertanda, where it spread out, made a waterhole, and flowed on. When they had thus transformed themselves into fully initiated men, the two, who were now grown-up men, walked about the country, performing the initiation rite upon different groups of men and women whom they met in the course of their travels. Amongst others they initiated some little bird people called Lintjalinga, whom they heard singing, and watched while they tried to circumcise themselves with a fire-stick. . . .[13]

The beautiful legend of the creation mission of the two brothers moves on with dignity to tell of their death by a waterhole.

After a time the younger brother said, "You and I are tired, shall we kneel down?" but the elder brother made no reply. Then the younger knelt down with his hands behind him, and after a time he said, "Shall we stand up?" Still there was no reply from the elder. They were carrying their *leilirra* in their waist-girdles, and had sacred *Churinga* [stones] under their arm-pits, on their shoulders, and in their hands, pressed up close against their stomachs. At last the big brother spoke and said, "We will neither kneel nor stand, but will lie down here. If we kneel or stand our Churinga will be seen, and then the place will be *ekerinja* (tabooed), and all the black-fellows will not be able to come and drink. Let us lie down upon them, and then they will not be able to be seen, and every one will be able to come and drink." So they lay down upon their Churinga and died, and two great stones arose to mark the spot.[14]

I have the uncanny feeling that through this story we may be looking down through the great void of the past to the point where man's humanity is marked by the simultaneous arrival of stone knives and the circumcision which would be impossible without them. It suggests that still more primitive people, possessing only fire sticks, looked with envy upon those who had achieved a higher technical level and received missionaries from them. Circumcision marks therefore, if this assumption is a reasonable one, a stage in man's technical advance. Before the use of knives, man's hunting must have been restricted to the food gathering of small edible things—nuts, fruits, grubs, small game which could be eaten with the minimum of preparation. Large game was useless except in so far as it could be torn to pieces with the teeth and the hands—and man was poorly physically equipped for this. With fire, some larger game might be broken down to an edible stage, but the technical difficulties in the way of capturing, killing and dismembering larger creatures must have been almost insuperable. The first stone knife transformed that situation. It may have made possible the killing of large animals. It certainly made it possible to dismember them. And it is an advance of the highest order for intellectual reasons too. Knife in hand, primitive man becomes a crude surgeon. He skins his game and uses the skins. His knives dismember carcasses, separating parts, and he learns his first lessons in bodily structures.

He exposes the most secret parts of entire creatures to his curious eyes and fingers. Perhaps it is on animals first that he learned the primitive surgery he practiced on his own kith and kin. But certainly the two advances came together; and when early man had learned to use his knives he must have recognized how much they separated him from the animals, and how far advanced he was over peoples still more primitive, who did not yet possess them. This feeling is implicit in the story I have related. To circumcise would be to advertise this human superiority over the animal. That is why it was the mission of the two brothers to transform the various beings they met into "complete" men, and initiate them by circumcision.

We must recognize, I think, that a sense of the sacredness of life breathes through this story of human origins. The behavior of the two brothers, knowing death upon them, and contriving to die in such a manner that they would not deprive their breathren of water, is in the highest degree comradely and unselfish, and movingly told. If we see in it man making his first technical advance, we see man already possessed of the highest degree of compassion.

4

When all that can be rationally said about circumcision, subincision and similar ceremonies has been said, we should be unwise not to recognize something dark in these practices. I am not thinking here so much of the magical and demoniacal aspects of primitive ceremony as about evil. There is a manifest love of cruelty in man, even self-inflicted cruelty, and the further we go back in human history, the less it is disguised. It is certainly present in much primitive ceremony, especially, of course, in ceremonies of initiation. The conclusion has to be drawn that the tribal old men enjoy the pain they inflict—though not simply wantonly, for it is a stern social duty too. But in the revolting developments of repeated subincision which certain aboriginal peoples practice, there is obviously an exploration of the possibilities of inflicting pain. It is perhaps (so little do we understand our human condition) even a mark of unconscious human genius, that tribal cere-monies rigorize the cruelty that man wills to inflict even on those near and dear to him and provide a periodic surrogate for man's cruel lusts. But even that rigorizing can itself become the excuse for further cruelty. To understand this we have to recall the long record of human sacrifice in world history, particularly perhaps the endless butcheries practiced by such as the Aztecs as part of the observance of religious rites, and of all that is implied in the legend of Abraham and Isaac.

Animals are not cruel. When we *say* they are cruel we mean that they are ferocious—they will fight to survive, or to triumph, or to kill, when they have to, with an unfaltering will. But to be cruel they would need to identify themselves with their victims, and that they never do, so a fox or an otter wantonly killing is simply work-ing off an excess of killing fever. It has no enjoyment of anything but its own power. But the man inflicting pain on another is in spiritual sickness, for that which is obsessing him is what his victim is suffering. He is identifying himself with his victim all the time and loses interest when his victim loses consciousness. So that if we admit that there is a strange sexual genius in the use of circum-cision and similiar rites of initiation in the solution of problems of tribal unity and identity, let us not endow savages with virtues of restraint and moderation sparse enough even among civilized peo-ples. In the very legend I have been quoting, the same Atnatu who showered upon men the gift of knives, in another story grew furious with men who failed to sound the bull-roarer loudly or sufficiently long, and hurled down his spears upon them, dragged them up into the sky, and ate one of them.

In the scriptural narrative, as I pointed out, the institution of the rite of circumcision of the newborn was part of the covenant with God. Abraham marked it by the circumcision of the whole male portion of his household, from the infant Isaac upward. It is fol-lowed immediately in the Bible story—and significantly, I think—by the visit of the three angels who received Abraham's hospitality. The promise of the Lord is renewed through them: "Shall I hide from Abraham that which I do; seeing that Abraham shall surely become a great and mighty nation, and all the nations of the earth shall be blessed in him?" [15] It is impossible not to note the connection between circumcision as a symbol of a painfully achieved national unity through the mortification of man, and the promises of future greatness. But this renewal of the promises of the Lord after Abraham's sign of his obedience is a prelude to the judgment of the Lord that Sodom and Gomorrah shall be destroyed. Abraham softens the judgment of the Lord by his pleas, but Sodom and Gomorrah are nevertheless destroyed by fire and brimstone, "because their sin is very grievous." Traditionally, the sin of the cities of the plain is sexual license and perversion. But a *special* mark of their sin was that they laid hands forcibly upon the angels of the Lord. This is powerful evidence that primitive societies discover unlicensed sex to be a sin not simply against the flesh, but against the spirit. It is seen to threaten the human condition.

The Bible records show how the compact marked by circumcision is strengthened as the generations roll on. Moses brings down the tablets of the Law. He fights wrathfully against what we can call foreign practices and ways, and strange gods, and social and religious values alien to the ethos of his own people. We see more clearly in the scriptural narrative than anywhere else the struggle to weld a people together against all the forces, internal and external, which work to sunder them—against the lures of practices ostensibly religious but in fact evil, against the consequences of conquest, or the economic and spiritual imperialism of stronger peoples, until finally the elaborate laws of Leviticus set a whole people "within a frame that binds them" and from which it is both antisocial and impious to seek to escape. Leviticus also describes the terrible disasters which can fall upon a people which breaks the will of the Lord. We can read this, at this moment, as a list of the kinds of forces which war against primitive society from its first establishment.

Leviticus 26 speaks of these punishments for those who deny the Lord: "terror . . . consumption and fever, that shall consume the eyes, and make the soul to pine away: and ye shall sow your seed in vain, for your enemies shall eat it. And I will set my face against you, and ye shall be slain before your enemies: they that hate you shall reign over you; and ye shall flee when none pursueth . . . I will make your heaven as iron, and your earth as brass . . . your land shall not yield her increase, neither shall the trees of the land yield their fruits." Plagues, "wild beasts which shall rob you of your children," diseases to destroy the cattle, and war and captivity are promised, until the cities are laid to waste and the sanctuaries "brought into desolation." [16] The catalogue is not a logical one. But if we consider it as a list of those things which a primitive society had most reason to dread, we must see it also as a list of disasters which a society tried to arm itself to forestall or defeat. They are, first, natural disasters such as fire, flood, drought, pestilence, and rapacious wild animals; the help of God may be secured against them, and a tried social solidarity would provide a weapon to endure or defeat them. Next come the hostile acts by other men —war, destruction, captivity and, finally, the loss of the homeland and the laying waste of its hearths and altars.

As we read the Bible, we see that the society so difficult of accomplishment becomes, when established, a matter of pride. The generations are counted back to Abraham, and the pedigrees of the righteous paraded. Proof of descent from the fathers is as much the mark of the covenant as circumcision. Even when we come finally to the life and mission of Christ, his descent from Abraham is recounted as proof of his righteous messiahship. One must not simply belong, one must give *proof* of belonging if called upon. Sir Arthur Grimble in *A Pattern of Islands* [17] gives a charming account of how it was the custom for the islanders when moving through the islands and coming upon new people, to give proof of belonging by reciting as part of their personal introduction their descent from the gods through the known generations; and he himself, in order to be accepted as one of them, had to have invented for him a pedigree which he had to recite as "proof" of his legitimacy.

The table of ancestry slowly becomes in human affairs proof of status, rank, tribal or social standing. It is the mark of blood kinship which cannot be taken from the possessor of it no matter what happens to him. It is only in democratic centuries that it has ceased to be of importance, yet even so, aristocratic claims in our modern world depend on it, kingship rests firmly upon it, and visitors to the Highlands of Scotland would be unwise to assume that it is dead. And we can easily see the role it has played in the maintenance of society, a role which becomes stronger when the forces of disintegration grow.

All that has been said in this chapter points to the importance of the effort to maintain the tribal identity; it has to be supported by a constant social effort, for it is not natural, not given, but a human artifact. It has to be maintained, first, against nature. Nature is terrible to the man who has escaped it, but stands only just above it. If the opposition of nature is strong enough, the society cannot survive. Then, too, there is the opposition of other peoples—their cultural, economic, military and spiritual aggression. Every strongly united people constitutes a threat of some sort to the peoples surrounding it. By military power or superior techniques or trading capacities it can in one way or another make neighboring peoples subject to it. But it may do none of these things, and still prove a menace. It may present what I will call spiritual imperialism, and Professor Toynbee calls cultural aggression. One tribe may permit action forbidden in another, or eat foods taboo in another, or worship as friendly gods which others regard as hostile. There is no aggressive intent in these practices—at least, in origin. They simply represent in their totality a different but equally valid pattern of life. The element of cultural aggression enters when one tribe or people discovers that another commits things on which it has set the seal of its disapproval. A conflict may result in which the ways and ideas of one tribe penetrate peacefully the life of another. On the other hand the penetration may be understood as a threat to tribal unity and resisted by war. We who, in the modern world, are accustomed to the conflicts and wars of opposing ideologies ought to find nothing strange in this. If neither war nor cultural penetration results, then we may have the situation in which both parties deliberately seek isolation one from another—an iron curtain in fact. The Australian aborigines who have never resisted the penetration of white man's civilization are dying out from the deep malaise which discouragement has brought. The naked Aucas on the other hand cut off contact with a flight of spears.

Threats to the maintenance of the tribe come from the inside too, from rivalries, jealousies, economic and political competition within the tribe. And so we find that the elaborately structured tribal society gives birth to an immemorial pattern of settling issues before they can destroy the people. Custom decides all, and the tribal leadership lies with those who have the right to decide wherein, in matters under dispute, the true path of custom lies— with those who have the greatest experience, in fact—the tribal elders. We, when we look back from the heights of civilization, find the rigid patterns and formulae of the past a framework which holds back the mind, which impoverishes the intellectual life of a society, and we disapprove.

But that is only because we are gifted with hindsight. Were we within such a society, we should see the pattern of rigid tribal custom as the only barrier to the fratricidal anarchy which threatens continually to destroy primitive societies, and which must in its time have led to the extermination of many of them. Among the internal stresses, the greatest must be sex—the jealousies within a tribe for possession of its women, the cultural influence of other tribes with different sexual mores. This is such an explosive force within the tribal life that it is subject to powerful controls which hold a delicate balance between restraint and license, and circumcision is a universal symbol of this balance.

CHAPTER five

SEXUAL ALIENATION

AND TECHNOLOGY

1

It is usually unprofitable to relate primitive societies to modern civilizations. An unspoiled tribal society is both ecclesia and tightly knit social group, bound by precedent, custom and belief into one sacred identity. The only sacred identity remaining in the modern world which is universal in the area it covers is the nation, but even the nation no longer receives the reflex loyalties which were once its right, and it has always been far more full of tension and conflict than the tribe. With the passage of a common Christian faith modern societies in the West are not only more sophisticated but more and more pluralistic. There is not one common morality and viewpoint on the world and on the nature of man, but many viewpoints, irreconcilably in conflict. One has to research into sociological and anthropological research itself to arrive at an overall notion of the social and sexual mores and religious attachments associated with class, income bracket, status group, ethnic minority. Even then, one has not done, for the evi-

dence of contemporary literature yields a picture of a vast, un-
happy personal ferment beneath the glittering, glass-curtained technological society.[1] The student revolts of the contemporary world
bear witness to the gap between the scientific successes and the
equally colossal human failures of society.

Contemporary society in all its complexity is indescribable. All
the same the obligation upon intelligent men is to understand it
and to describe it as far as they can.

The limitation the theme of this book imposes—to understand
how society contains sex—does not much simplify the task. Not
only is a modern society, and particularly its great accomplishment,
technopolis, pluralistic in its sexual mores but the pluralism can
obtain in one street, or in a single family, between different generations and members of the same generation; between one church
and another and members of the same church. Moreover, the
sociopolitical, the scientific-technological patterns and programs of
society deeply affect all our sexual lives and our efforts to understand and play out our sexual roles. Modern society has no rite of
passage comparable to the rite of circumcision in tribal society.
Nothing initiates a modern child into the personal and social controls required of his sex in so dramatic and public a way. I once
argued that the only equivalent rite of passage in the modern world
was leaving school and going to work.[2] If that assertion is true
then initiation into an economic role has taken the place once
occupied by sociosexual maturation. The remaining rite of passage
then is purely secular and expresses only the traumatic moment
when a child is old enough to sell his labor. That is itself a comment on the sad triumph of the "economic man."

The theological world, over recent years, has been in confused
and excited uproar over the conception of *secularization* as an explanation of what is happening to the modern world. The theme is
most vividly developed in *The Secular City* by Harvey Cox,[3] which
sang (theologically) the praises of technopolis as the mega-creative
act of the twentieth century. Not only in this view was the metropo-
lis a huge accomplishment but it promised a new kind of man,
liberated from the mythologies which bound him in the past, mythologies about work or race, religion or sex, a man who had at last

fulfilled the divine commandment to have dominion over the earth
and over every living thing. Here finally was man come-of-age, the
truly secular man, who though far from meek was going to inherit
the earth. The supreme role, perhaps the only role, left to Christianity was to celebrate this.

Typical of the new city were anonymity and mobility. For Harvey
Cox the symbols of the secular city were the cloverleaf highway
and the giant switchboard. It isn't necessary to subject this hubristic
theory once again to the analysis I gave it in *The Death and Resurrection of the Church* [4] but simply to mention that the sometimes
magnificent (and sometimes not) achievements of megalopolis mask
the other social process so marked in our times, and against which
Negroes, students and workers riot, burning the secular city—and
that is alienation.

2

Marx, of course, spoke of the alienation of the worker from
his labor. His labor became, not the source of his individual or
social creative achievement, but a commodity like any other commodity bought and sold in the market. He "sold" his labor. It now
belonged to someone else. The product of his labor was no longer
his. Under the division of labor he contributed a minute fraction of
effort to the construction of some final product he might not ever
see, or understand, let alone want to buy. As for the recognizable
but anonymous products of manufacture, he would queue in the
market for them like everyone else. Not simply was this an injustice
for Marx, it was also a humiliation, even a dehumanization of man.

The secular city is not only created by this very alienation. It
also fosters it. For the alienation which begins by separating a man
from his labor ends by separating him from many or most of the
decision-making processes which affect him. On the one side are
all the millions of anonymous people at their daily work, on the
other all the vast powerful institutions—plants, research institutions, financial institutions, government departments, universities—
in the inner webs of which decisions are made by no one quite

knows whom, decisions which are often irreversible, often unannounced, sometimes uncomprehended, and in that sense fatal, perhaps for the whole of humanity. This alienation of the ordinary man from the centers of decision making and organization motivation is patently the case where societies are run by monolithic, remote communist parties. It is true, more subtly, more deceptively, of democracies too. How to end it is the great political problem of our time.

The alienation of man from his labor, from his power of decision over his own life, is completed by his alienation from his sex. In what sense are we to understand this? It can be argued that Freud and Jung make this their theme, Jung in the argument he advances about man's denial of the dynamic urges of the collective unconscious—for "denial" we could read "alienation from"—and Freud in the importance he attaches to the Oedipal point of transition in infancy. Whatever happens in that transition, the sex life of the infant is transformed. If the transformation is not completely successful in moving the child on to a more mature discipline, then the person is permanently alienated from his sexuality and its normative outlets. Homosexual, lesbian, pervert, pederast, fetichist, sadist, have *by nature* (and by the will and approval of society) an aboriginal sexuality which seeks a fulfillment biologically directed and socially blessed. If that can never be consummated, and if in other respects those who suffer this situation are normal, responsible persons, then what we stand faced with is alienation rather than pathology. If the sexually alienated praise and propagate their condition, then they resemble the prisoner who kisses his fetters. As the sexually alienated grow in numbers (and it is probable that they do so today) so the general sexual alienation of society grows stronger, and man in that degree dehumanizes himself. All societies produce sexual casualties—Freud denounced the monstrous social superego which crippled sex—but technological society just by those peculiarities I have described maximizes them.

As if that were not enough there is another source of sexual alienation in the social phenomena I have been describing. The anonymous masses are in a peculiar way an atomized people. The political phenomenon of the Soviet Union illustrates this in an extreme form—a few powerful leaders (or just one) on the one side, the faceless, voiceless, powerless, propaganda-fed masses on the other. The leaders are most powerful when the led are most afraid of each other. In that sense society is atomized, its corporateness in any independence of the leadership deliberately destroyed, the lonely crowd created, the spontaneity of social emotions atrophied, human warmth replaced by a cultivated coldness and withdrawal. But what happens deliberately under a cruel regime happens as it were inadvertently in Western societies. A man is nearly always seen in his function—schoolboy, student, clerk, political boss, production-line worker—and it becomes difficult to see him in the round. It is usually as an assemblage of functions that he is viewed when he has to be treated medically, rather than as a psychosomatic whole. There is therefore even a predictable inner atomization, a dissociation in the man himself as between, for example, his working self from his thinking, feeling self; his sexual life from his gender life. The dissociation of sensibility, the affectlessness, which results from a compartmentalized life has been regarded by some thinkers as the special disaster of our technopolitan culture. It is the theme of Erich Kahler's rich study of contemporary society, *The Tower and the Abyss*.[5] It means the loss of power to identify with other people, to enter into their sufferings and joys. It is a failure in the capacity to love, destroying those who should love and those who should be receiving love. It cripples society in the very dynamic which has created society.

As one example of this glacial affectlessness he takes the wartime tragedy of the little French town of Oradour-sur-Glâne. Because of supposed support for the resistance, which turned out not to be true, the whole town was reduced to ashes, the entire male population shot and, according to Ernst V. Schenk,[6] "all the women and children locked up and burned in the church. If such a thing had been done in a delirium of hatred, aroused by a savage fight, it would have been gruesome enough, but somehow humanly understandable. But the Elite Guards who had received this order . . . carried it out with utter calmness and placidity." They not only assembled the women and children with marked kindness and gentleness but hugged and fondled the children, played and joked with them, carrying them lovingly in their arms or placing them carefully in perambulators. "The mothers were moved by so much tender care on the part of these dreaded men" and followed them confidently into the church as if to a festival. "After all the women and children had gathered in the church the doors were closed and the mass murder began." The executioners were the same S.S. guards who had brought them there.

Here the dissociation of sensibility was complete: the guards were atomized beings without a unifying manhood. The agents of this affectlessness had become machines. In *Five Chimneys* [7] Olga Lengyel, herself a doctor and an ex-inmate of Auschwitz-Birkenau, told of surgical experiments on women and boys. Among them was irradiation of selected subjects to discover the effect of X rays on the generative faculties. Boys so sterilized were forced to masturbate or forcibly masturbated by a metal instrument to discover the vitality of the spermatozoa. She speaks, among other experiments, of a thousand boys between thirteen and sixteen used in this way, then sent to the gas chamber. The affectlessness itself was mechanized.

The accounts of these crimes of our time are endless and all point to the spiritual death of their perpetrators. They were committed often (and certainly the medical experiments) by cultured men and women who afterward went home and kissed their loved one, said prayers with their little ones, and went peacefully to bed. Such affectlessness and on such a scale speaks of the death of a whole culture.

If this curious atomization is even in part responsible for the alienation of man from his inner self we should expect to find it at work in less criminal but not less anonymous societies. Perhaps it is to be seen in the mindless, conscienceless violence of America, that assassination-haunted land: in the *Playboy* attitude to sex, in which sex becomes just justified fun, divorced from its social content; in such literary straws in the wind as *In Cold Blood* by Truman Capote, which is indeed cold-blooded writing—the author's clinical identification with the murderers vastly comes to exceed his sympathy with the victims; in the vast, pullulating pulp pornography industry which gives one really the sick sense of what it means when capitalism sets out to exploit a market.

But pornography is a lonely business. It is the sex of the solitary. Its very success as an industry points to the lonely sex life of the lonely crowd. With the gender role lost in society, and sex irrelevant to function, sex life can be nothing more than the moments of orgasm, the pursuit of it a movement from orgasm to orgasm— which so many young today demand as an inalienable right—rather than the continuous developing gender role of which orgasm is only one part and the fruit of which permeates and enriches the whole of life and makes sense of sex. However, the full sexual alienation, even its transmutation into rage against sex, will be clear only when we look at the evidence of literature.

3

Alienation has still another aspect. It is of the nature of the technological and organizational aspects (over against the personal and familial) of our metropolitan society that it is sexless in the ways I shall presently describe. It has "use" for sex only in a production-line sense as a need to be serviced or as a commodity to be bought and sold. It services sex coolly and efficiently through fertility and contraceptive pills and devices, abortion techniques, aphrodisiacs, maternity wards and so forth. It turns sex into a commodity, not only in the obvious but limited sense of male and female prostitution [8] but in the exploitation of the market for sexual fantasy and for vicarious sexual and sexo-sadistic experiences for commercial profit, and finds its most ready victims and proselytes in those sexually alienated from society. The extent of the sex-commodity industry is probably incalculable; but the evidence of this ruthless exploitation of human lasciviousness and sexual hunger is omnipresent—it ranges from the pulp magazines to nudity films, from shopgirl romances to the leg shows of the tabloid press and up to the highbrow films which publicly display copulation. Even an attempt to estimate the situation is confounded by the fact that the line between brave and honest handling of sex by writers and others sick of hypocrisy, and the commercial exploitation *even of them* is a very thin one indeed.

However, the point is not to discuss the form and propriety of this exploitation but to single it out and to insist that the conversion of sex into a capitalist-exploited commodity has something of the same significance for alienation as the conversion of labor into a capitalist-exploited commodity. It degrades sex and isolates it. The subfusc solitary males endlessly watching nude shows or films in Soho clubs symbolize this fate. The little adolescent boy in Angus Stewart's *Sandel* suddenly weeps for the pointlessness of orgasm under clothes. For much of the vicarious, commercially exploited sterile sex of our times one is required to weep. The alienation of sex means, of course, its externalization into something you can buy, or indulge in, or, as Mary Quant said, something you can take or leave alone, like a gin-fizz. It ceases to be your being-in-the-world.

Earl H. Brill in a firecracker of an article,[9] "Sex Is Dead," took up Marshall McLuhan's point that "every new technology created a new environment which translates the old environment into an art form," and applies it to the changing sex ethos.

When sex was truly a total preoccupation, our major concern was to become free so that we could express ourselves sexually. We tried to fight repressions, inhibitions and conventional restrictions.

But in recent years, sex has become an art form. We buy quantities of how-to-do-it books; we construct models of Adequate Sexual Behavior and try desperately to conform to the images we have constructed. The development of sex as art form probably reached its culmination with the recent publication of *The Human Sexual Response,* by William H. Masters and Virginia E. Johnson (Little, Brown), which describes in meticulous detail how the sexual act is carried out, how the body temperature changes, the pulse rate increases, the muscles tense. Imaginative writers have frequently described the accompaniment to heterosexual genital activity with such phrases as "her pulses quickened" or "he was sweating like a stallion." Now we are given chapter and verse, number and sequence. Now, perhaps, we can construct from the data the Perfect Sex Act and get it preserved for all time in silver at the National Bureau of Standards. Or perhaps, if it is to be generally accepted as a true art form, the model ought to be exhibited in the Museum of Modern Art.

In *Christian Century* also, Robert T. Osborn wrote in "Sex and the Single God" [10] of the theological process of "sealing religion's womb"—that is, of the loss of biblical sexual realism. "The Bible contrasts the creative, redemptive initiative of God with the receptive, humble response of Israel. Yet for all the differentiation God calls Israel to be his wife and to enter into a radical unity or covenant with him. Husband and bride, different yet one in marriage."

He accuses the new theology of a share in the annihilation of sex, and therefore of Christian fullness.

A dominant trend in modern theology, most consistently expressed perhaps in the writings of Thomas J. J. Altizer, is to speak no longer of a covenant between two but of a "coincidence of opposites." Man, rather than finding God "out there," objective and different, now finds his alleged opposite inside, as "coincident" with himself. If I may, I would say that the knowledge of God is no longer a matter of intercourse but of masturbation. If, as Nietzsche suggested, we posit ourselves faithfully and long enough the eternal will recur. J. A. T. Robinson invites us to look for God not out there or up there but within, in the "depths." Bonhoeffer saw the thoroughgoing sexlessness of modern theology and addressed himself to the problem when he asked how the church can speak of God to a world that does not need an other; God is as relevant to a godless world as is a groom to a sexless bride. Following Bultmann, Robinson would rid religion, by a program of demythologizing, of all objectivity, would as it were seal religion's womb. Unlike Mary the modern church is not receptive.

There is shrewd perception behind these engaging polemics. For all that belongs to the technopolis of which the symbols are the cloverleaf highway and electronic switchboard sex is meaningless. Sex is not to be found in the heart of the power structure of technopolis itself which more and more is served by sexless robots, and to understand the technopolitan indifference we have to look at the peculiarly functional nature of modern Western society.

4

The ticket collector at the barrier, the conductor on the bus, the cash girl in the supermarket, the cashier in the bank, the policeman on crossroads duty, perform well-defined, self-evident *functions* in society. There are thousands and thousands of such sharply delimited functional performances throughout industry, commerce and government services. Some have already been taken over by the machine—the crossroads policeman has been replaced by traffic lights—and some (the ticket collector, for instance) will soon be made redundant by mechanical devices. The fact that this transposition can be made reveals a degree of mechanism in the repeated human act which is the basis of the service. Our society has in this sense become increasingly functional and in the same degree depersonalized. The typist who belongs to a large office pool may take her place in a vast hall, which is actually a typing factory, put earphones on her head and type what comes out of the tape recorder or intercom. She may never meet the executive whose disembodied voice daily reaches her. This is not all. The executive himself may impersonally serve an impersonal organization the sources of whose power and authority through the hierarchy of other organization men are obscure to him; he is hardly less of a functional man than the ticket collector, even if not yet mechanized. But he may be one of the intermediate executive group whose tasks will shortly be delegated to the computer. When he shuts his office down at five or six he moves into another, personal dimension of living with no connection with his daily job. All this is absolutely typical of the organized, urban man throughout the world; and the dichotomy between personal life and socioeconomic function is there too.

It is in part necessary to our complex society that this should be so. Confusion, delay, anarchy, loss, would result from the effort to transform impersonal functions into personal face-to-face relations. Trying to "chat-up" the cash girl in the supermarket on her, or the ticket collector at the barrier on his, personal life (with a queue behind!) would add enormously to the frustrations of many more people than the two functionaries concerned. We simply have to accept that many urban tasks can only be fulfilled under the incognito of anonymity.

Yet, though the executive, the worker, the typist, may have adequate compensation for a faceless socioeconomic role in family, home, friends, the depersonalization of society can bear very painfully on those whose life is personally impoverished, who are deprived people, or casualties—failures, the old, the lonely young, the sick or ailing, the housebound, the immigrant, the ghetto populations, the migrant worker, the very poor. And as society grows more and more functional what could become extremely serious, even schizophrenic for society, is the gulf between the vast dehumanized world of apparatus, organization, cybernation on the one hand and the life of hearth and home it sustains.

We might relate the growth of the functioning and impersonal society to the theory of the division of labor first propounded by Adam Smith in *The Wealth of Nations* where with much eloquence he described the number of processes appropriate to the manufacture of a pin and the natural division of labor this called for. Since his day the manufacturing world has conscientiously pursued the doctrine that the more finely the processes of manufacture are divided, the more this allows for speed and the development of higher skills. At its peak a worker tends to contribute one repetitive function to the whole labor process. This can be true of a society still manual. The machine just rationalizes and standardizes the process. It can be the machine which will do the actual work, threading the screw or spraying the bodywork with paint, while the worker only controls or "minds" the machine the skill of which has become faster and more accurate than his own. The whole productive process everywhere tends to get more and more broken down into minute, exact stages terminating with the finished product. We can reach such a degree of rigor and invariability in the process that we can take the men away and hand the process over to cybernetics. The cybernated plant renders even a supervisor watching dials or a handyman wandering around with a grease pump redundant. The plant's own information feedback triggers off the appropriate internal responses to check all unwanted development. Such a rationalization could not succeed unless everything was standardized, the idiosyncratic disposed of, the nonfunctional stripped away. The computer itself, symbol of the functional society, is the product of precisely the same logic of one step, and one step only, at a time, with all that is irrelevant excluded.

5

But then what is true of industry grows more true of society generally, though it is harder to describe. The expert, the town planner, tends to look at society not for what it is but for what it does. It is what is happening, and what ought to be happening, that interests him—where the traffic is coming from and where it is going and how the city can be organized to bear its load. And so the streamlined motorway takes the place of the rambling lane, the traffic circle and traffic lights replace the motoring free-for-all, rails, and pedestrian crossings act as conduits for those who still remain on their feet. With an instrumental precision the planner would, if he could, measure the flow and the growth of *future* society. It is so important that future populations shall be provided for that we hand over even our environmental present and future to the technologist. Cities get zoned functionally because only in this way can they be managed; industrial, residential, shopping, recreational zones are created—sometimes university and hospital zones too. Almost everything gets involved in technological decision making, fewer and fewer things happen haphazardly or of themselves in the public sphere. In taking over, the technologist is compelled to think functionally—what is the exact nature of the service required, how best to provide it? What is the contribution of this or that institution, building, street and so on? I have no intention of speaking of this in an alarmist way. The pace of growth in modern societies is such that things cannot be left to chance. Chaos is always around the corner. Free enterprise societies have not been conspicuously successful in social provision. But the contrast between the organic society growing at its own pace and resistant of change and the modern engineered society is nevertheless a stark one, for the new society inevitably limits individual decision making, subjects the individual to external controls—in the interests of X he shall be made to live at Y, in the interests of Y he shall be removed from Z, in the interests of Z, he shall . . . and so *ad infinitum*.

The functional conception of man and society invades education too. I do not mean this in the sense that we use language laboratories and closed-circuit television, though this is important, but that education becomes more and more a matter of acquiring exact skills. J. H. Plumb's symposium, *Crisis for the Humanities*,[11] has acquainted us, if nothing else has, with the unhappiness of the arts men and the confidence of the scientists. The question Professor Plumb's team in fact raises is: What is a general education in the humanities good for as against the technical know-how science demands? Perhaps the fragmentation of much research happens in obedience to the computer logic of one fractional step and only one fractional step at a time. The ambiguous role of religious education in schools is additional evidence. What is the relationship of religious education to other subjects which are taught rationally and analytically with the intention of producing skills which can be examined? Religious education does not normally invade their sphere, but the spirit of rational inquiry frequently invades religious education. Finally, of course, the I.Q., the notion of which has dominated selection procedures for much of the century, has nothing to do with character or spirit or courage or perseverance; it is purely a mental function or skill measured according to its efficiency and speed and used to determine (for the masses only) the right to higher education.

Certainly, the functional, the engineering conception invades the biological, at least in the sense that man has more and more control over his biological functions and extends control over more and more species (reducing or exterminating some insect populations by sterilizing the males, for instance). The human body and its functions tend to be treated as engineering, or chemical engineering systems, the deficiencies of which can be overcome by the provision of internal or external spare parts or corrective drugs. Of course this process is as old as medicine itself. What is perhaps new is the feeling for the plasticity and malleability of the whole body so that man may not merely correct what goes wrong but in a degree redesign it. The lengths to which this development has gone are quite startling to the layman. It would be an ingratitude to quarrel with a medical progress which has so greatly alleviated human suffering, increased longevity, and almost eliminated some serious diseases. But it would be wrong not to see in this a changed attitude to human life, a certain dissociation of sensibility about it, so that it is now looked upon as material as accessible for experiment as any other. An individual's rights over his own life could become inferior to the claims of medical research.

6

The handing over of human lives to provide the raw material of advanced medical research was first openly perpetrated by the Hitler regime. Then Jews, gypsies, imbeciles, crippled children, death-camp prisoners, became medical fodder, as we know. Dr. H. M. Pappworth, in *Human Guinea Pigs* [12] lists many examples of research conducted in British hospitals on patients from whom no consent was known to have been obtained, or was obtainable, and argues that they were based on the principle first advanced in all its severity by doctors under the Hitler regime, that the pursuit of new scientific discoveries must override consideration of human rights or medical morals. He relates among many cases in Britain the example of eight patients suffering from gastric ulcers who were subjected to experiments in lumbar aortography which involved stabbing a large needle six inches deep into the spinal column in order that the aorta and its branches could be observed on X-ray screens. The experiment had no relation to a cure of their trouble; it was purely an opportunity to practice a difficult skill. Three of the eight patients died. In another experiment described by him twenty-one mentally deficient patients, purely as an interesting piece of research, "had been given a meningitis."

In an experiment in 1963 concerning oxygen consumption in paralyzed men exposed to the cold, three patients were concerned.

The first was a paralyzed polio patient, aged thirty-four, kept alive by respirator, the second a patient of sixty-eight, unconscious for three months from operational shock and brain damage, also kept alive by respirator; the third was a patient aged seventeen, unconscious for twelve months from severe head injuries.

The basic metabolic rate of the first subject was studied without the use of drugs and then again while he was receiving a dose of tubocurarine (a drug which causes paralysis of muscles including the respiratory muscles). All the subjects were made to breathe oxygen through a closed-circuit apparatus and also received amounts of tubocurarine. Observations were made for forty minutes while the subjects were recumbent and covered with blankets.

The blankets were then removed and fans played cool air over them for eighty to two hundred and ten minutes, during which periods observations were continued. The subjects were then covered with blankets and warmed with a "heat cradle" and the observations repeated.[13]

It is not so much that the research students obviously regarded these three people as useless living lumber but that they achieved that dissociation of sensibility of the kind the jailer has to the jailed, the executioner to the condemned, the airman to the far-away enemy, the thief to his unknown victims—that these are proper material for his skills and for whom he has no responsibility, and with whom no identification. It is a divisive process alien, one might suppose, to an organic society but built into a functional one.

There is a possibility that the whole human race, not simply its helpless hospital inmates, could become the raw material of the physiologist and geneticist, with incalculable consequences. Professor Joshua Lederberg, Professor of Genetics at Stanford University, described in *The Bulletin of the Atomic Scientist* [14] how, in a future nearly with us, it may be possible to multiply identical twins indefinitely. The reproductive cells in human beings are created by halving the number of chromosomes in the normal body cell. When spermatozoon and ovum unite in the zygote the combination of their chromosomes brings the number back to the norm. This process of reduction and restoration ensures that the new human being shall possess qualities, good or bad, deriving from both parental stems—that it shall in fact be a new, unique human being, for the very fact of cross-fertilization rules out absolute identity with the parent. But, Lederberg explains, a new genetic technique has been demonstrated with frogs. It is to take a nucleus from a *body* cell (which would necessarily contain the full chromosome count) implant it in an ovum from which the nucleus had been removed, and place it in a womb to develop. There is now no cross-fertilization. The embryo possesses an exact blueprint of the body from which the nucleus has been taken; it will develop as an identical twin of that body. A thin paring of human tissue would provide innumerable cell nuclei. One conceives (granted the available wombs) an army, even a race of "identical twins" or "clones" as they have come to be called. It is rather like propagating the human race as one propagates a rosebush, by cuttings. In fact, Lederberg describes the "clone" technique as "vegetative propagation." In his definition, "A colony of organisms derived from a single ancestor by vegetative propagation—without sexual union or genic recombination as a step in the process." And he argues that it threatens the definition of man on which our culture rests. The idealist, or the eugenist, dreams of the perfectibility of man by such processes. One propagates Einsteins, Beethovens, Socrates, Churchills. One can imagine regimes (Need one imagine? They are already here) which would wish to use the clone technique to multiply janissaries, or replicas of Hitler or Stalin; and others, of such exquisite silliness and emptiness, which would wish to produce only nubile sexual dolls of both sexes. And cannot one see the husband who wants only a succession of girl children made in the image of his adored wife or of doting sons every inch their father? As formidable is the possibility of human genetic material introduced into animal ovaries to produce a subrace or a mosaic race intelligent enough to be permanent human slaves, but not intelligent enough to threaten it, Calibans by the thousand, differing from one another only by the number they bear branded on their flesh. A science fiction dream? One wonders. The techniques are almost with us.

7

Of course this is a functional invasion of the sexual. The reproductive functions are separated from the social and emotional nexus in which they normally operate, objectively refashioned and made to serve a production-line view of reproduction. But the principle is not new, only (in this fantasy) the extent to which it is pushed. I have already spoken of the fact that we have powers of artificial insemination, fertility pills, contraceptive pills and pills to delay puberty. At any moment we may discover means to pre-determine the sex of an embryo. Most significant, in Britain at least, is the steady (statistical) extension of abortion. The Act of 1967 extends and regularizes the grounds of legal abortion. The legislation was debated in terms of the most liberal and humane values; its intention was—is—to prevent the misery of unwanted births in overcrowded families and for unlucky young unmarried girls. But what it unwittingly establishes even more firmly is the right of living human beings to dispose of unwanted new humanity *after* its conception, to determine in creatures who are living but not able to plead their case, their right to exist. It is therefore the expression of a new power doctrine, probably soon to be used against the aged, that those at the height of human maturity have a right to dispose of inconvenient sections of humanity. It is the right to feticide, which is scarcely removed from infanticide. It is clear that the sexual in society is here regarded as something just as necessary to control technically as other social functions. The form of control is a further step in the dissociation of intercourse from reproduction.

Already this takes us far from what we might call an organic view of sex and society. To my Victorian grandparents sex issued in childbearing and there was no escape outside personal restraint from the annual pregnancy, and this restraint was the more difficult to achieve the poorer you were. It was conceived to be the inescapable human condition—the price paid for living at all. So much so that Malthus could not discover a human, or humane, regulator of population growth—only famine, war and disease. It was the death rate alone which kept populations stable. Such is still the condition of half the human race and of all other species of creatures. It is the biological or organic inheritance, and the kind of technical mastery we are now asserting over it removes it and is intended to remove it from its position as a basic social determinant to just one of many desirable human functions allowed to operate only under certain controls. Of course the process is a liberating one, as any escape from an external necessity or fate must be. But do not let us regard it as a return to a simple natural sex of Mary Quant's brave new world. It is primarily the invasion of the sexual by the nonsexual, the determination to put sexual activites under the control of nonsexual values—values of social interests, or individual pleasure, of privacy, freedom, or living space.

Research about it is often also part of that invasion by nonsexual values, as illustrated in the works of Kinsey, and Masters and Johnson. The introduction which Kinsey writes to *Sexual Behavior in the Human Male* [15] is full of charity and understanding. It is not for the investigator to take a moral line. At the slightest sign of horror or disapproval the interviewee shuts up like a clam: "Nothing human is alien to me" has to be the investigator's motto. (But the stance of sympathetic listening is often a kind of moral identification). It is impossible to read Kinsey's meticulous account of interviewing techniques without realizing that the investigator is a kind of seducer. His plans, his steps toward it, are craftily worked out. Unlike the man-about-town in "Diary of the Seducer" it is not the entrapment of a sixteen-year-old girl, but it is the baring of a human soul. The goal may be the lofty one of human knowledge, but there does remain the question of the entitlement of any one individual to so deep an invasion of the privacy of another as the Kinsey—or the Masters and Johnson—investigation demanded. True, the complacent answer is that the clients are not compelled to reveal their cases. But, as with door-to-door salesmen, this is precisely where the art of seduction comes in. Never, in any case, Kinsey said, ask them what they do. Assume that they do everything and ask them when they first started.

He lamented that public opinion was not ready for the laboratory tests and experiments relating to intercourse and orgasm, but his own work changed the climate of thinking about sex in America and prepared the way for *Human Sexual Response,* the clinical study by Dr. William H. Masters and Mrs. Virginia E. Johnson, who watched, charted, measured and analyzed (other people's) sexual activities in their laboratory, with an insolence of which only the most humble scientists are truly capable, and as though their own motives could never be suspect even to themselves, and the value and meaningfulness of their knowledge was beyond question. Even the assumption behind this kind of research is a functional one. It is that the investigators in their professional role can be impassive and impassible while those investigated will show severally all the quirks, vagaries and irrationalities of human nature, and that once the white linen coat of the professional voyeur is taken off the investigator will cross the line into the investigated world, of which he will form once again an irrational unit, unaffected by his professional objectivity. That a man can be one thing in his professional function and dissociate *himself* from it in his private life is at least one aspect of what I mean by functionalism in society; it is also one of the characteristics of alienation. A high dissociation of sensibility in *investigated* people might be reasonably regarded as pathological by those very professionals. What are they to say of it when it occurs in themselves?

8

One suspects that something strange is happening to human society, in the West at least. I find it hard to describe except in terms of that dichotomy at the heart of Soviet society at which we have looked. There, as we saw, one's private life is one thing, the public life another. The values one lives by in the family and with close friends are the negation of values publicly declared. One lives to one set of values, works to a totally contradictory group. It is possible to do this without breakdown only by the compartmentalization of one's life: the public and private are not allowed to break into each other. Both Boris Pasternak's *Dr. Zhivago* and Alleluyeva Svetlana's *Twenty Letters to a Friend* [16] illustrate this central dilemma. Indeed, for Alleluyeva Svetlana, the public domain is almost completely absent; Russia, except as landscape, is missing from her book. Necessarily so, perhaps, because the portrait of the father fondling his favorite child while drowning Russia in blood is finally unbearable just by that very dissociation. It is the world of the child murderer who puts on his best suit and brushes and pomades himself and goes out and kills his little victim and comes home, washes and brushes himself up, puts on the kettle, and loving and moist takes up tea and anchovy toast to his invalid mother in bed. It is the whole ethos of the Nazi death camps, as recorded by so many anguished eyewitnesses.

How does one explain it? The scientist in his rigorous objectivity detaches himself from what he observes. He looks out upon a world of things and energies which is quite other than the world he lives in. And this will be true even when the things and energies of the observed world are social, political and economic forces—human beings, in fact, viewed in special categories or functions with the ultimate intention (of course) of manipulating them in those groupings or activities. I wrote once [17] that the tragedy of contemporary Europe sprang from the doctrines of man it had consciously and unconsciously absorbed from its science and its political and philosophical speculation. I instanced the evolutionary view which regarded all living things as expendable, and nothing as enduring in the unending struggle for the emergence of new, finer, more triumphant species. In a universe of flux the living individual counted for nothing except for his contribution to some unknown, far-off triumphalist evolutionary destiny. Translated into social Darwinism, this meant the acceptance of the struggle for existence within societies and between nations and of a view of man as an expendable scrap of living material rightly manipulated in a cause which utterly transcended him, a cause to which he owed duties, but against which he had no rights. This was at the root of the Nazi doctrine of race and folk, blood and soil. When I wrote *The Annihilation of Man* I did not in fact know that on the basis of this theory the Nazis had exterminated six million Jews and hundreds of thousands of nationals of other races. Of Marxism I said that it substituted class for race but still regarded an individual as having rights only as a member of a class, and a right to exist only as a member of a *dominant* class. Both doctrines presented rulers with a theoretical justification of the extermination of members of society they regarded as undesirable. I tried to show, in as many ways as I could, that society molds its institutions and its laws around the doctrine which it holds of man (recognizing that some societies are pluralistic in their doctrines, and that no doctrines are clear and watertight).

All doctrines which reduce the status of man would seem to be schizophrenic. Doctrines which see man as the fuel or fodder for economic or evolutionary processes would seem to exclude the proponent or manipulator of the theory. He is the one who sees, who understands and on that basis controls *other* people. His objective understanding places him outside the field of investigation, just as it does the scientist. He will live and want to live his life in the private sphere of free choice, while others will live theirs in the sphere of the historically or biologically determined. If it is a political tyrant we are contemplating, then *those others* will move along the tracks his will determines.

One hesitates before the possibilities of exaggeration yet it does seem that what has been politically attempted under the banner of Marxism in Russia and China and their satellites and National Socialism in Germany may be accomplished technologically (and obliquely) in the world. The poet Charles Péguy spoke somewhere of *capitalistes d'hommes*. He meant the demagogues, the party leaders, the political bosses who built up power by their hold over men in much the same way—hoarding, investing, spending men— as the industrial capitalist did by his command over material resources. But the day of both types may be over and be succeeded by the human engineer, the capitalist of techniques, the methodical planner.

The Professor of Experimental Psychology at Sussex University, Dr. N. S. Sutherland, writing in *The Observer*,[18] said, "We are on the verge of a revolution in the conditions of human existence that will make the industrial revolution seem trivial by comparison. In 50 years' time the world will be unimaginably different from today. The change will be brought about by advances in our knowledge of how to process information. Just as the industrial revolution led to our replacing the energy of our own muscles with other forms of mechanical energy, so the computer revolution will lead to our substituting the intelligence of machines for that of our brains."

It used to be the dream of eugenists and social Darwinists—a dream not yet dead, as the "clone" theory of reproduction tells us —that man would presently be surpassed by a superior species, a superman, a biologically perfected man. But it occurs to Professor Sutherland that he will be bypassed by his own machines.

"There is, indeed, no obvious upper limit to the intelligence of a computer. To make it go outside the limits of the problems set by man, it would of course be necessary to build into it certain goals such as intellectual curiosity. Once this is done, computers will be able to look for new problems to solve, as well as solving the ones we put to them. In fact the next step may be the development of such machines. *The human race may be superseded by its own artifacts.*" [19] He explains that many unsatisfactory human biological features arise from the "survival value" element in evolution. However, if it is not necessary to build personal survival or even propagation of the species into computers, elements of aggression, selfishness and irrationality will be absent from their makeup. "This means that computers may be the first true saints." [20]

In *The Rise of the Technocrats*,[21] Professor W. H. G. Armytage has given us the anatomy of the new class which will run the computers from its first beginnings in the "plantocracy" (those who botanized and gardened and brought us tea, tobacco and potatoes centuries ago) to the modern (if I may be forgiven) Einsteins of industry and Fords of science, in a book of painstaking erudition. What he has really described is the rise of a new scientific culture to dominance over the whole world and the glacial flow of the technocrats into the seats of power. A good thing? Ortega y Gasset saw technocrats bursting like barbarians onto the political stage like demons through a trapdoor. And more modest commentators have spoken of "the impersonal, non-ideological, relentless and possibly overwhelming impact of technology on government." The shape and complexity of megalopolis, the motor saturation, the vast computerized production plants, the obsessions of an age of space probes and military rocketry, give us fair warning of the new kind of life that is swallowing us up, which Professor Armytage describes as "An Operational World" and which Professor Sutherland expects computers and other robots to control. Armytage makes perfectly clear one point—a mass-production age mass-produces technicians and scientists too. Are we to see in them the new helots or a Wellsian Samurai? Are they the new Prosperos or Calibans —or some horrible crossbreed of "Pralibans"? He quotes Clark Kerr: "Certainly never in history has knowledge been so central to the conduct of an entire society." But it is the knowledge of a pragmatic engineering kind which alone counts as knowledge in a positivistic society. Oswald Spengler wrote: "I can only hope that men of a new generation may be moved by my book to take up engineering instead of poetry." Beyond the grave he may be consoled. They have.

Lewis Mumford takes to pieces the goals of the society we have been considering in his magnificent *The Myth of the Machine*,[22] and Armytage summed up the challenge of his book in a review he wrote in *The Guardian*.[23] "Mumford is now giving us, if not a map of hell, some very clear warning signals that it lies ahead. Unless man 'minds' as well as 'makes' he is going to crucify himself again, for who can entertain the prospect of a passive, purposeless machine-conditioned man committed to the pursuit of technology as an end in itself?"

However, I must not allow consideration for the fate of human society to deflect me from the theme of the role of sex in our modern world. Is it devalued, trivialized, in the kind of society we are building, or does it find its true role, its natural *métier*, at last? Can we possibly know?

SEX AS AN IRRELEVANCE

1

When I reflect on the society I have just discussed I am struck again by the irrelevance of sex to its functioning. Just as it can make use indifferently of a human or a mechanical agent, so too it can make use indifferently of an agent of one sex or the other. There is hardly a point in it where sexual differences matter at all except where they affect technical skills. Where they do, industry capitalizes them. It makes use of men in roles involving hard muscular labor and of women in roles involving neat, intricate operations and small repetitions. Even this is not an infallible division. The Soviet Union consistently uses female labor in heavy industrial operations such as mining and road making; it is the capacity of the sex, not the sex itself, which is the determinant.

Certain jobs are customarily filled by males—police, miners, steelworkers, engine drivers, soldiers, politicians—but this in part reflects traditions which are a hangover from male-dominated societies. All such roles have been invaded by women, particularly in times of war or crisis. Under economic pressures the importance of the sex differential seems to disappear. Technically all that many tasks demand is the skill and there is not much physiologically between the sexes in skills, granted equal opportunities in training. As the demand for brute manual labor decreases, women's economic equality is bound to grow. But a functional society in which equality between the sexes grows apace is also an *asexual* society. It is indifferent to the sex of the agent it uses (costs being equal) so long as the tasks set can be fulfilled. No one is sexed or desexed by his or her socio-economic functions. At the same time fewer and fewer socio-economic roles contribute to the fulfillment or enrichment of a person's gender.[1]

In Joy Adamson's *Born Free* [2] (and in the film based on it) we are given an insight into the socio-economic relations of the sexes in a pride of lions. It is the role of the lioness to make the kill, to drag it to her mate and to step aside while he eats his fill. Elsa, brought up in a human society, was quite ignorant of this etiquette, and when set free and having found a mate, she killed for her own hunger, she was badly mauled by her mate for failure to maintain the "pecking order."

Down through the ages most human societies have been as deeply divided sexually as the lion pride. The gender division was not only made clear and instantly recognizable from the moment that this became socially important to the growing child, but it provided the basis for the total organization of society. The bisexual nature of society was sacred. To the women clearly defined economic tasks—field labor, cooking, washing, cleaning; to the men hunting, fishing, war, trade. To the men, the making of knives, bows, tools; to the women, the making of pots and clothes, the preparation of hearths, the collection of kindling. The division of social functions was often as clear. For the women the care of infants and the aged, the training of girls, the supervision of pregnancies and childbirth. To the men the training of sons, the participation in councils and rule, the organization of rites of passage, the transmission of tribal lore and law, the maintenance of relations with neighbors, the showing forth of tribal grandeur in dance and display.

SEX AS AN IRRELEVANCE / 95

It is difficult for us in modern civilizations, where just about everything is discussed in the open and everything gets changed under our noses, to understand how the bisexual order appeared to an established tribe as firm and as sacred as the natural order. Indeed the tribal order was the natural order; a break in the first had repercussions in the second and vice versa. So much was the bisexual tribal life taken as given that a tribal male could not do women's work without becoming a woman in the eyes of the tribe, compelled to wear women's clothes and live with them and behave like them. The American Indian tribal male who could not accept the pace of the male life in a stoic warrior community retired to the squaws and became one, to all intents and purposes. Maleness so conceived is not a matter of physiological characteristics but of socio-economic function within the tribe.

A reminiscence of this comes down to our own day in Western society. In its farming communities the farmer and his wife have always fulfilled clearly distinct economic roles—the farmer, master outside; the wife, mistress inside. To the farmer belongs the care of stock, the plowing, sowing, reaping, the buying and selling, the hunting, the control of hands; to the wife, the whole interior economy, furnishing, cleaning, sewing, baking, curing, the kitchen garden, the henroost. It comes down to us in the homebound Victorian housewife whose husband punctually left for the office at eight and returned home at seven. It lingers on today in the same division of functions as between husband and wife. Where the wife stays at home and the husband "works" they perform still in different socio-economic dimensions, each a separate world of skills, contacts, and understanding. Desmond Morris, in *The Naked Ape,* traces this role playing back to man in his first primate stage when the emerging human community functioned at two levels, the hunting cooperative of males and the hearth-minding, child-caring group of females.

By deliberate social policy in the West male careers have been opened to women. By deliberate political policy women have been given the vote, and educational opportunities have increasingly opened to them. The doctrine behind these reforms is that, despite the primatial difference, women are as capable as men of functioning on what was previously the male side of the bisexual society. Of course, this is one of the crucial decisions of modern society, the significance of which is that it lifts both sexes onto a plane where they are expected to function nonsexually, transcending their sex as citizens and as persons, as if they had consummated the union of opposites which is the theme of Plato's *Symposium*. It is a Christian theme, that we hold a person to be a value in his or her own right and not merely as the agent or vehicle of his or her sex. In the history of civilization it does seem that one significant contribution made by Christianity has been the endowment of women with spiritual rights.[3] It appears, in the record book, as the lifting of women to equality with men. But the meaning of the accomplishment is the discovery of a plane which both men and women can enjoy as persons without their sex counting either for or against them. What modern society may be moving to in the most liberating of its developments is the structuralization of this profound Christian quest.

The sociologist would accept other kinds of evidence today of the movement of men and women into the same socio-economic dimension. In young families today there is a blurring of roles in the rearing of quite young children. The young working-class husband is no longer so committed as he once was to the Andy Capp world of pub, football game, and the dogs; he may stay at home to help with the shopping and the "do-it-yourself" decorations. The Sunday with cronies becomes the Sunday with the family in the car. Like his middle-class or even aristocratic opposite number, he may handle the washing up or even the cooking. As households become increasingly mechanized so his role in the repair and supervision of the home machines grows more important.

Yet all this has another meaning for the wife. The home which is more and more a partnership is less and less a personal burden and social restriction. Husband and wife are released for other things. Home machines reduce sheer physical labor. Families in the semi-detached tend to be nuclear, with two or three neatly spaced children and no grandparents. The children are brought together to maturity. With increased longevity, these reductions of familial commitments can free many women from perhaps the forty-fifth year on: they are offered a generation of life and work after childbearing as the kind of nonsexual socio-economic person we have been discussing. The great-grandparents of this generation, on the other hand, believed that life was over at forty.

The new technological society carries everything forward impetuously in its stride and changes the relationships between the sexes. Women cannot be kept out of that technological world. Their skills are needed there as much as men's, and the appetite for skills is so far unsatisfied. But the world in which men and women operate more and more on terms of equality (or more accurately on terms of equal acceptability) is itself an asexual world. There is no tradition within it of a relation of its products or processes to one sex or the other. Even that there is a biology within it is hardly known to its operatives. The manufacture of sugar, the distillation of gasoline, the processing of plastics, the smelting of steel, all move to the same type of impersonal mechanistic operations. When one passes into the world of computers, telecommunications, cybernetics, rockets, nuclear physics, one has reached a plane where sex has total irrelevance. It is a world of such mathematical rigor that sex has no more meaning to it than to the angels. The only entry to it is expertise. Of its importance, on the other hand, there can be no question. This asexual world holds our human destinies in its fleshless hands. It is symbolic that so much of its ironmongery rises above the stratosphere.

Speaking, in *The Myth of the Machine*,[4] of the sexual one-sidedness of monasticism, Lewis Mumford went on to draw a parallel between the economic value of sexlessness in monastic days and at the present time. "In later developments the divorce between the factory and the office on one side, and the home on the other, became as marked as that between the earliest archetypal bachelor armies for war and labor and the mixed farming communities from which they were drawn. The lesson of the anthill, that specialized work can best be done by sexual neuters, was increasingly applied to human communities, and the machine itself thus tended to become an agent of emasculation and defeminization. That anti-sexualism left its mark on both capitalism and technics. Current projects for artificial insemination and extra-uterine pregnancies reflect it."

I spoke earlier of man's continuing efforts to escape from the tyranny of the reproductive cycle. One aspect of this is man's increasing control of the biological on which I have touched; another is the subjection of human life, and of human sex itself, to other disciplines. Is what we discern in the technological society a continuation of that enterprise, or a qualitatively different enterprise?

Of course, the long process of disciplining or civilizing sex continues in our time and in our pluralistic societies but takes forms far different from the tribal rites of passage and taboo systems. But like those forms, it places sex at a distance—at arm's length. Language, clothes, culture patterns, literature, laws and customs, internal and external censors have the task of maintaining the distance, the control, so that the other values inherent in the individual and the social life may find expression. A monastic pattern of life expresses almost dramatically the intention of shutting off its adherents from a sexual life which would destroy the struggle for a celibate goodness, that is, for an alternative cultural dimension. But this kind of task belongs to any civilization as much as to any tribe.

What is *different* in the secular, technological civilization of our times? Precisely the uncontrollable expansion of that relatively new realm of human technology to which sex is actually an irrelevance because it has no place there and nothing to contribute. The technological enterprise does not have to set sex at a distance—it does not acknowledge its existence. The sex of workers, directors, research workers has no place in that clinical world. Unless it happens that sex is being investigated or exploited, it is of no interest. Talking computers, androids, have no sex. That men and women meet and operate in this asexual dimension and function the better there if they can act as if they had no sex is not a denial of sex, but constitutes a temporary banishment of it. But precisely this is the necessary condition for the enlargement of this sphere. It grows and grows in modern society, supporting an elite which finds fulfillment through it, but doubly alienating those whom it simply uses.

This sphere of the technological can never become coextensive with the whole of man's life. Short of reaching the test-tube society of *Brave New World* and the extinction of humanity in *1984,* there will remain the arena of warm-blooded human beings, loving, hating, bearing children, creating families, struggling to defend their personal and social standards from every encroachment. The peculiar nature of modern society presents them with a double task. They have, like all their forebears, to discipline their own sex and rear their children in that discipline for the sake of their civilization. But they have to do that in a technological society which dismisses the sexual, is incapable of sustaining and dramatizing gender roles, and vulgarizes sex itself, when it touches it, by turning it into a commodity, or an object of clinical investigation.

We have to try to see what happens to sex under these pressures.

CHAPTER seven

THE FAMILY AS
THE MASTER PATTERN

1

Whatever analysis we make of contemporary society, it is still true that the biologically given family remains at the heart of society. Remarks such as Dr. Edmund Leach's in his 1967 Reith Lectures that "far from being the basis of the good society, the family, with its narrow privacy and tawdry secrets, is the source of all discontents," display a profound contempt for its nurturing role. The pair bond, the maternal and paternal ties with the young during their long immaturity, all the lifelong relationships set up in this socio-biological way, constitute the material on which all societies raise themselves, and some would say religions too. One might speak of the family as humanity's master pattern. It is true that it is the container and promoter of aggressions and tensions (can we imagine that they would be less *without* the family?), and we need only to go to any welfare worker's casebook for evidence, but it is also the liquidator of them, the instrument by which, through face-to-face relations and loving acceptance, parents may grow in human understanding and children pass through all their traumas of development at last to their own maturity, their emotional and spiritual independence. The psychoanalytic evidence makes us acutely aware of what happens when children do not make this long and arduous passage to maturity, but it sometimes makes us forget that most children do make it, sound in wind and limb and psyche, at least to the degree that society itself is sound, and having in themselves the power to redeem society.

Though no society has succeeded in destroying the family (Chinese society has tried to subordinate it to the commune and dying elements in Israeli society to merge it into kibbutz) societies do variously interpret the family, stretching it to include all relations and to give uncles, aunts, grandparents highly significant roles in childbearing, property control and marriage contracts, or narrowing it to the immediate biological family of parents and offspring, as British society with its managed family has now almost succeeded in doing.

These facts remind us that a family is never only a biological unit, it is of necessity of economic unit. The responsibilities involved in the nurture of children can be assumed only if the provision of food, warmth and shelter is first met; these provisions in their turn demand power, skills, property. The breadwinner must have the right and opportunity to direct his energies to productive ends. It is possible for the biological family to function as this independent socio-economic unit. There are times in every society when it must. But what, delving back into history, we so often meet is not the biological family, which is too weak and small a unit to assert itself in a complex society, but the extended socio-economic family—a Scottish clan, the French bourgeois *famille,* or something like Abraham and his sons and grandsons, slaves, herds and encampments—the tasks of which ramify away from hearth and cot into the intricate legal forms, property rights and productive modes of society itself.

This socially extended family protects and supports the biological unit in society. If the need for that support shrinks (as in a welfare state) one can understand how it comes about that the socially extended family loses significance and the biological family gains it. In a non-welfare state, care of the aged is the concern of the socially extended family. In a welfare state the burden is shifted to the state; so too are many other of the problems of the biological family—childish sickness, parental illness or poverty, childbirth and its costs, homelessness. In a society in which property owning is widely diffused the socially extended family becomes an important managerial group, protecting, preserving, increasing and passing on property which is truthfully group rather than private property. In a communist society, where only the state owns property, or in Western capitalist societies where only a few have capital and the rest have trivial possessions (such as houses, which have no productive role) the socially extended family loses its role. The point is that the role and influence of the family rises and falls with the forms and aspirations of society as a whole, extending imperially along all lines of kinship at one moment, shrinking to the biological unit at another, *but it never disappears*. And in whatever shape it appears it is the channel not just of the physical rearing of the child, but of its social and religious tutelage. Of course, this includes that teaching of sex and related behavior patterns which society as a whole approves.

2

The monogamous family in Western societies is the institution where sex in the sense of intercourse, or entitlement to intercourse, is "established." Here alone it is lawful and even obligatory, if the marriage is to be consummated. The offspring born in wedlock have legal standing and legal claims upon their parents, just as man and wife have legal claims upon each other. These legally recognized ties are not simply social and familial but economic too, as any man finds out who deserts his wife and family. Even into marital sexual activity the law has not hesitated to intrude and, in the light of Christian teaching, declared certain forms of eroticism unlawful and ground for divorce. At the height of Victorian puritanism every form of sexual activity or relation outside the marriage bond was morally condemned and usually subject to legal sanctions too. Even where, as in Latin societies, the brothel or other forms of prostitution were tolerated, the justification usually given was the protection of marriage and of the virtue of women of good repute from pressure and assault. Men had to be allowed a legal outlet or the safety of society was endangered. Even so, the legal brothel was usually kept under severe restraint, licensed and medically inspected. British society has never tolerated it, not only because it encouraged sexual license but also because it allowed the exploitation of the bodies of women for profit.

Less than a century ago Britain was roused almost to the point of riot by the revelation of William T. Stead of the *Pall Mall Gazette* and Bramwell Booth of the Salvation Army that a virgin girl could be bought for £5 for immoral purposes and that a profitable trade existed in such luckless creatures. The British compromise—to refuse to legalize prostitution whether private or through brothels and to keep it under by prosecuting streetwalkers—has never worked satisfactorily either from a legal or a social point of view. But the point here is that the suppressive legislation was intended to help to contain sexual activity within the marriage bond. "The sanctity of home and family" was a phrase often on Victorian lips. It was not just hypocrisy. The marriage bond itself was subject to prohibited degrees of consanguinity, the tables of which once adorned all our prayer books. And the law severely punished incest, rape, homosexuality, sexual assault, assault of minors of either sex, or carnal knowledge of them, irrespective of their consent. Alex Comfort in *The Anxiety Makers*[1] retails with some relish the Victorian campaign against juvenile masturbation, a practice argued to produce madness, degeneration, impotence, senility and pimples if unremittingly pursued, and his book provides illustrations of metallic contrivances, equipped with spikes and electric alarms, to be worn by children as medieval women had to wear chastity belts, a lunacy one imagines limited to an eccentric and hysterical fringe of middle-class society.

Comfort seems to regard such eccentricities in much the same light as the war between mineral oil and constipation waged by Sir William Arbuthnot Lane, but the campaign against masturbation was not the invention of a few crazy doctors (though it is true that some exploited it) but an expression of the deep anxiety of society about uncontrolled sexual activity. The more it is *felt* by society that sexual activity should be restricted to those relations which can be legally defined and understood, and seen to be beneficial to society and its institutions, the more intolerable grow all other sexual activities. They are judged to be morally and socially threatening—tempting men and women away from their proper sexual roles and destroying familial and social relations. This is as true of a Victorian anxiety about masturbation as of the Trobriand people's dismay over incest. It witnesses to the deeply rooted idea that the sex of an individual belongs to society and must operate under the rules of society—autoeroticism gives nothing to society and, operated in secret, unfits the culprit for a sociosexual role. That is the unspoken concern. It is even and properly a witness to the basic human anxiety. One might put it this way: in sexual activity the biological will of the species takes over from the personal will. Every man—and therefore every society—has the constant problem of foreseeing and guarding against a takeover destructive of other valued human relationships. Mankind has the right and duty to be anxious in this, the superego sphere. I was going to say that it is the price man pays for his society, but reading Desmond Morris's *The Naked Ape* and understanding from him the development of the monogamous pair bond, and the need to safeguard the wife with her young from the attention of other males while the husband was hunting with his tribal group, convinces me that we have to recall the theme of Chapter One— a deep Kierkegaardian *angst* about sexual activity is the *pre*-condition of being human. There is no human society which does not have to face the problem of sexual control; it is a tribute to the depth of the anxiety that some systems are so elaborate as almost to defy description. When a society shifts its sexual balance from, say, excessive puritanism to excessive promiscuity, this is not necessarily to be regarded as a "liberation," but rather as the product of an excessive unease, of the difficulty of finding a norm between restraint and freedom.

3

Sexual activities are not the only biological functions to cause the family anxiety. The first indeed are the sphincter controls in infancy. Standards over the disposal of feces and urine, and degrees of tolerance over their noisomeness, vary from society to society, of course, but every society appears involved in a struggle with its infants to bring them to the level of sphincter control and excrement disposal society regards as proper. Once the child reaches an age when it can understand what is wanted, control is achieved in a variety of ways, such as by coaxing, bribing, the giving or withdrawal of love, the example of older siblings, punishment. Even banishment if all else collapses—the child who finally fails to control bowel or bladder movement is barred from the family nest or bed which he might foul. Even the most primitive family understands that not only comfort and standard of living is involved, but health too. Deliberately an intense anxiety about this is generated in the child in order to rouse in it the will to control its functions (this buildup of the will is one necessary function of anxiety). If control of evacuation of body waste is not established, then adult life in most communities is made impossible. I once listened to a police court case of a middle-aged man found sleeping on a grating over a bakery. He had no address and no means of subsistence. He was a confirmed enuretic and no institution and no lodging could cope with him and he could get no job because he stank. Indeed failure when not purely physical (or senile) is regarded as evidence of psychological disturbance. That it is so regarded is evidence of the degree of importance (the degree of anxiety) society attaches to this control: it is almost the condition of entry into the human community.

A second discipline is over the intake of food. A breast-fed or bottle-fed child may be fed when its cries show that it is hungry. But in the end some regularity has to be established for the sake of family order. It cannot always be fed when it is hungry. It is sometimes fed when it is not. The will of the baby must not always prevail. Even if the mother is willing to accede to all the baby's demands she is not always in a position to do so. The external world imposes its own timetable. Jobs, shopping, the needs of the rest of the family, the garden, the washing, hospitality to visitors, all can prevent instant attention to the baby and lead to frustration of its will. When the time comes for the infant to feed itself yet another discipline has to be met. Meals cannot appear as magically as breast or bottle. There has to be a table discipline, a pecking order. The infant has to be restrained from throwing food about, messing itself totally, wasting food, breaking plates or heads.

These are only among the first demands the familial world makes upon the child. Others follow, or accompany it. It must submit to being washed, bathed, cleaned; being dressed; dressing itself; adapting itself to the bedtime and getting-up order; controlling its aggression against other children; learning the difference between the indoor and outdoor order (their demands in relation to clothes, behavior, intimacy, for instance); discovering the familial ramifications—after the discovery of parents, siblings, it must learn to know uncles, aunts, grandparents, with their different degrees of family acceptance and authority. From the familial it must pass to the exploration of the external world and its inhabitants—streets, shops, school, postmen, policemen, schoolteachers—learning to shut the door on one world before entering the next.

Freud, in his concentration upon infantile sexuality, sees a crisis, the famous Oedipus complex, in the child's relations with its parents round about the fourth year. The child has to come to terms with its own sexuality and to accept only a share in its mother's affections, moreover one subordinate to the father's rights. The male child must simultaneously accept the father as a character model. There follows a long period of psychical and physical sexual latency. One can describe the process as the end of the supremacy of the id and the coming into existence of the superego, the instrument of anxiety, disapproval, suppression. But it could be, as Erik H. Erikson seems to suggest in *Childhood and Society* [2] the emergence of the ego as the balancing mechanism between id and superego, the protective force which wards off the excessive and excessively dangerous demands of either. "Between the id and the superego, then, the ego dwells. Consistently balancing and warding off the extreme ways of the other two, the ego keeps turned to the reality of the historical day, testing perceptions, selecting memories, governing action, and otherwise integrating the individual's capacities of orientation and planning. To safeguard itself, the ego employs 'defence mechanisms.' . . . The ego, then, is an 'inner institution' evolved to safeguard that order within individuals on which all outer order depends. It is not 'the individual,' nor his individuality, although it is indispensable to it." [3] And he goes on to study a schizophrenic child (a case of ego failure) and then the significance of play. He takes up a case of child play described by Sigmund Freud himself.[4] The boy, eighteen months, deeply attached to his mother, was forced to be without her most of the day. He did not on that account rebel, or become naughty, but developed (in Freud's interpretation) his own form of compensatory play. He would hurl into the corners of the room or under his cot all the toys or little things he could lay his hands on—no light task, Freud says, to gather them up afterward. And this with expressions of interest and gratification, and a cry Freud translates as meaning "Go away!" The child had a spool with a string attached to it and holding the string the boy, making his "go-away" noise, would throw the spool till it disappeared among the bedclothes, then retrieve it with a joyful exclamation "Da!" ("There!"). He learned to play a similar solitary game of disappearance and retrieval, this time of his own self before a mirror. Freud saw in these games re-enactment of the daily trauma of the little boy's loss of his mother—the daily drama of disappearance and retrieval.[5] But he was not just enacting it, he was using objects under his control to master the experience, to incorporate it into his ego, to adjust his life to it. In Freud's phrase he was turning passivity into activity. The spool on the string was his mother whom he forced to go away, then as easily recovered. Of course, such solitary, compulsive play does not change the external situation. The mother still goes away.[6] In this case, Erik Erikson explains, "Our little boy, however, told his mother of his play, and we may assume that she, far from being offended, demonstrated interest and maybe even pride in his ingenuity. He was then better off all round. He had adjusted to a difficult situation, he had learned to manipulate new objects, and he had received loving recognition for his method." [7] The ego would seem to be at work here as adjuster and compensator between the id and the external reality as early as eighteen months.

I select this case specially to illustrate the traumas of development because it was not an Oedipean situation. It was not a sexual situation, but the mother-child relation, the "imprint" relation, in which the mother is necessary to the child's existence, and loss of the mother is deprival of that other in which the child is mirrored; it is physical rejection, loss of security, of love. It is characteristic of hundreds of situations through which a child must pass from birth onward to its own maturity and beyond. Indeed many of the infantile traumas of loss and rejection and denial of love are experienced again in age. Some psychologists assert that the intrauterine experiences and the birth difficulties themselves create traumas which mark the human character permanently. The rearing, body training, social and formal education of the child involve a constant delicate balancing on the part of the child. It must itself adjudicate between its own will and appetites and the need for security, recognition and love; between itself on the one hand and the external familial world from which most of the satisfactions will come, on the other.

4

We have not yet looked at the sexual problems of a child's nurture. But enough has been said already to show that a child's sex must appear in modern society too as a psychosocial gift, a power which society awards rather than a biological inheritance. In that excellent book *Male and Female,*[8] Margaret Mead discusses the many ways in which different primitive peoples nurture their infants, and in *Childhood in Contemporary Cultures* [9] continues the analysis for contemporary societies. Margaret Mead shows how simple differences in nurture produce in their turn different sexual behavior systems, producing sexual confidence or timidity, clear or confused sexual understanding, and bear strongly on the total cultural pattern. I cannot rehearse all her examples, but one spoke of the loving readiness of the mothers of one people to suckle and cradle the infant at the breast. The breast was always available to suck; the child had only to be passively there for everything to come to it—warmth, affection, food, transport. The role demanded of the infant was pure passivity—any protest or activity might endanger the child's place at, or in, the external womb. This appeared fine for the female child's development, since passivity, expectancy, dependence, were traditional elements in a woman's sexual and social roles, but what of the young male complying with and enjoying this passive dependency in infancy? He has to struggle to discover and assert his sex and can never be quite as certain about it (or as reconciled to it) as his sister. His nurture did not confirm it.

Yet on the other hand, in societies where his maleness is made much of, praised and petted, exhibited, his penis pulled by the old chaps, he is being awarded a virility he does not actually possess and may never, he feels, grow to in terms of equality with the grown-up males around him—how can he be sure he will ever be their physical and sexual equal? Or what of the infant seldom nursed, always set at a distance and compelled to endless aggression to get attention? All his subsequent relations can be tainted by a sense of distance from people, from his own sex, only to be crossed by aggression.

The point is that these children in primitive societies may receive their sex as a glorious gift, then grow anxious as to whether they can ever fulfill the demands made on them, or they can have their sex muted and disguised, hidden and even perverted, and then struggle to discover what it is and how psychosocially to affirm it. If this is true of tribal peoples one can see immediately what kind of problems arise from nurture in highly clothed societies, where perhaps boys wear girls' clothes in infancy, and human physiology is carefully concealed. Or in our own society where sex is at once a highly private part of private life and a crude public commodity.

In Western society there is not to be found one universal pattern of nurture; but for that very reason there is no single social mechanism (such as tribal initiation) to help the young find and assert their gender. One has only to rehearse this material to demonstrate again the difference between the natural order and the human order. In a biological sense human sex is hardly ever in question, but its psychosocial maturation is permanently in question. In nature, the biological equipment dictates precisely the social behavior. Man has almost reversed this. The social ethos dictates the acceptability or otherwise of the biological powers.

CHAPTER *eight*

THE SEXUAL LATENCY
OF THE CHILD

1

Before we pursue the theme of the civilizing of the child and his or her sex, we have to make a distinction between civilizing and socializing processes. It is not an easy distinction to make but it is central to this thesis. A child in a Nazi youth organization was certainly quickly socialized, but not necessarily civilized, perhaps even decivilized. He was adapted to the norms of his society but these could be—and in his case most certainly were—alien to the civilization of which he was part. I am asserting therefore that a civilization is deeper and older than any particular society which grows out of it, and that there is a recognizable Western civilization, a Christian, humanist, natural law civilization struggling to survive. This civilization constitutes the infrastructure of any particular society and is concerned with the whole orientation of men —beliefs, principles, metaphysics, cultures—while any particular society is a power structure which could be beneficial to the civilization or destructive of it ("a band of brigands encamped on society," as Jean Jaurès once said of the dictatorship of the proletariat). Regimes such as the Churchill and Kennedy regimes at their height seemed essentially illuminating and civilizing. The Stalin, Hitler, Mussolini regimes precisely illustrate the argument about brigandage.

The theory I have been outlining bears a resemblance to the Marxist theory of the state as a superfluous social entity. At least the distinction Marx made between society and state I would tend to make between civilization and society; I would sharply distinguish between the two: it is often necessary to struggle against a society in order to save the civilization. The contemporary U.S. society and the tyrannical Soviet society are examples of societies whose present trends are inimical to the survival of Western civilization. The secular technological society in which we are living is in many of its aspects—inhuman scale, the dictatorship of economic costing, alienation—hostile to the civilization which fostered it. My concern for the civilizing of the child and its sex runs deeper therefore than the mores of contemporary society; it has to be related to older, more lasting cultural trends, as far as they can be understood.

2

The infant makes a hard journey to maturity. Alex Comfort said somewhere that a child has learned (or presumably mislearned) its gender role by eighteen months. The abundant childhood casework and psychoanalytic material collected in the last fifty years demonstrates that a point of emotional stability has to be reached quite soon by the infant. The child has to be held in a relationship on the loving side of discipline, and to know that it is so held. Without that love it may never itself prove able to love in maturity.[1] But there has to be discipline, even self-discipline, in which a child becomes able to counterbalance its own demonic rages at frustration and neglect against the sense (it does not have to be conscious sense) of the reliability of parental provision and family security. It has to reconcile its basic distrust and fear against its need to trust and to love those on whom it depends. Everyone has witnessed terrible infantile rages, which in an adult would send us rushing for a straitjacket, hushed to a comforted sob by the appearance of the mother. One sees, and catches the breath at seeing, a kind of decision taken, as though the child had said to itself, "I was wrong to fear. I ought to have known that she would come."

We see how deep the trust can go in the baby tranquilly sleeping in a pram, or in its mother's arms, in the traffic and pedestrian confusion of a great city, in an airplane take-off, or even in a traffic accident. On the other hand the breakdown of trust in an infant faced with sudden and inexplicable loss, the shattering of the environment or the withdrawal of love can bring devastating personality changes. Erik H. Erikson has explored them in *Childhood and Society* [2] and John Bowlby in *Maternal Care and Mental Health*.[3] A withdrawal into autism or schizophrenia seems even to the observer a refusal to live. The wound could hardly strike deeper.

The damage can all be done before the Oedipal stage is reached. There are those, such as Dr. Frank Lake,[4] who seem to regard the pre-Oedipal stage as more significant than the Oedipal in the self-making or self-marring of the child. Such thinkers look back into the fetal stage and the birth passage, hazardous or simple as the case may be, as decisive in the formation of the child's nature, since it fixes for all time what we may describe as the terms of its entry into the open world.

Yet for most of us the disciplines are learned, the familial role is discovered, the taboos imprinted and the knowledge of the outer world we collect is safely contained within the already burgeoning inward life. In the pre-Oedipal existence we come to terms with our dependent life; in the post-Oedipal existence, with our independence. First we come to terms with our sexuality, then during the latency which may last even as long as ten years, with our asexuality. The psychophysical and psychosocial value of latency for what we might describe in Teilhard de Chardin's terms as the child's hominization is felicitous. Erik Erikson speaks [5] of the crucial exteriorization of a child's life during latency. It has mastered locomotion and its own organs, and its conflict with its parents, and now can build its body-mind unity, its psychical confidence, on the acquisition of skills, the mastery of tasks in that external space it begins to explore with fascination. Achievements here render more immediate rewards in pride and self-regard than the unfruitful and exhausting Oedipal conflicts of infancy. Besides, mastery promises entry into the mysterious grown-up world in which people are swallowed up and delivered back by the unexplored space beyond the front door. Fantasies of technical mastery now appear. Every step or curb or rail or climbable tree is seen as a physical challenge. The tiny Andean savage stalks about with miniature bow or spear, or sets traps for sparrows. Spanish boys knock together wooden horns and play the role of bulls and bullfighters. The Western boy zooming about the gardens and pavements on a cycle or with arms extended as wings becomes the air pilot or astronaut, the ideal hero, the power symbol of his civilization.

The turning away from hearth and cot and mother's lap (which must stay *there,* available for fleeing to) toward action and achievement are obvious enough in the boy. A not dissimilar process is observable in the girl's passion for mastering the tasks of home-making (though the masculinization of the small girl in Western culture sends her into the camp of the small boys too). Sometimes she fulfills her longing, becoming, in a mother's sickness or absence, the "little mother" with real dependents, manifesting her satisfaction in her solemn absorption in running a home.

The turning of energies away from interior conflict into struggle with the problems of the physical world is so strong that the child even appears to drain himself of interior life. The love-demanding infant is turned inside out. Love scenes, tenderness, in films or on television, appear sloppy and mawkish to the pre-teens boy. The word *love* arouses a jeer. Caresses are greeted with coolness. He avoids and condemns girls who stand for no need as yet emotionally recognized in his life.

In his epigenetic theory Erikson pairs the industry of latency with inferiority. The child tries to compensate for his obvious inferiority by attempts at mastery of adult technology, and to overcompensate for his necessarily frequent failures by Walter Mitty fantasies. The locomotor drive in it all is unmistakable. There develops a curiosity about the world, unrelated to sexual interest, and a will-to-power just as asexual. It is this whole pre-teen orientation which makes possible and effective the sexual silence of latency. The act of turning away from sex, which is often blamed on parental shamefacedness or prurience or verbal inhibitions, belongs quite properly to the entire latency period. Because the child does not move on to sexual maturity at the Oedipal stage, it is suspended for several years in physical and emotional immaturity. It hesitates and is inhibited before that which it is not yet able to understand or experience physically or enjoy emotionally. So too its parents hesitate and are inarticulate before childish innocence and unpreparedness. Society seizes upon this valuable fallow period for the child's education and discipline. It reinforces latency by thrusting the child into that world of knowledge and skills, of technological discovery and environmental mastery which in Western culture is nonsexual or asexual and not to be comprehended in sexual terms. The importance of this in some cases is that a quite young child will be introduced to accomplishments around which he will build his whole life. One thinks immediately of infant geniuses, child prodigies such as Mozart, Yehudi Menuhin or William Temple, archbishop's son playing at being an archbishop at the age of nine, or Benjamin Britten composing furiously before the age of twelve. But it is not necessary to be a genius to be established in a socio-economic role before puberty. In Eastern civilizations today and in all societies in the past only the most privileged children escaped being settled in a craft or occupation long before puberty. It was not the industrial revolution which introduced child labor. Down the centuries the herdboy and the goosegirl have been as familiar as the newspaper boy is to us today.

Even if childhood is seen more self-consciously today as a period of life with its own rights and needs [6] and the child's labor is no longer exploited, it may still be true that a child is settled in the interests, skills and ranges of activity which will dominate his or her life, including the sport in which he or she will ultimately become professional. It is puberty which has to be adjusted to *them*.

The child is already subjecting his (or her) life to codes, roles and disciplines which have nothing to do with sex before his (her) sexual powers are fully aroused (one thinks of a child actor, a little girl model, a champion girl swimmer or dancer, a boy seminarian in a Roman Catholic seminary or a boy chorister—a professional at the age of eleven—in an English cathedral). All the pressures of society support them in this, and would *seem* to support them if they decide, as well they might on the evidence, that only this, the sphere of the nonsexual, is meaningful and important.

3

Instead of speaking of this in the abstract we might look at the development of the sexual and the nonsexual life in the years of latency of one of the most gifted and candid men of our time—Sir Victor Gollancz, who has left us several autobiographies.[7]

Gollancz tells us that as a very little boy he fell in love with geology.[8] It began by the discovery in his mother's bureau of a tiny duodecimo textbook with some enchanting illustrations. Soon he was progressing to more difficult textbooks and beginning his collection. Though ignorant of the sciences with which geology was linked,

I nevertheless developed an odd expertise within the range of my own capabilities. My appetite for detail was immense. I not only knew, as a matter of course, what genera of fossils were to be found in the various strata: I might also know, and always wanted to know, the name and appearance of a particular species characteristic, say, of some band, perhaps only an inch or so thick, in the chalk of Dover or the limestone of Bath. To unravel the whole story of the earth's past: to find that seas had been here, land-masses there, mountains somewhere else, at this or that moment in mundane history: to visualize the appearance of the changing populations—the echinoderms and ammonites and belemnites and lepidodendrons and ichthyosauri and dinosaurs and palaeotheres and mastodons, down, in types that teemed, to the smallest variation in the latest sub-species—it was this that so fascinated me, so compelled me to go ever and ever forward and learn ever and ever more until at last I should have won, as I passionately desired, the last guarded secret of the stony record. I haunted the airy galleries, aromatic with bees-wax, of South Kensington; I pored over show-cases with pencil and notebook, and made feeble sketches, now of some tiny bivalve, and now, moving on, of the vast megalosaur that bestraddled the length of a neighbouring room. Breaking off, I would eat my sandwiches in the grounds, on a seat by the stump of a fossilised tree, and then go hurrying back to my sketching. South Kensington Station, when nowadays I happen to pass through it, brings back to me, always, these holiday expeditions: airiness, and bees-wax, and summer afternoons.

Someone brought him the two-volume standard work of Sir Archibald Geikie when he was thirteen. Experts at South Kensington Museum aided and encouraged him and admitted him to the geological library there. He joined the Geologists' Association at ten or eleven—the youngest member—and was not prepared to enlighten the family when they confused this with a Fellowship in the Royal Geological Society.

Here is precisely the exteriorization of a childish life in the period of latency in the pursuit of genuine expertise—a pursuit zealous, happy, uncomplicated, releasing—on the part of a sensitive and highly intelligent young person. Fortunately for our case he has also spoken, though briefly, of the growth of his sexual consciousness in the same period.

In *My Dear Timothy* he explains that he had his first sexual experience at the age of nine, as Rousseau did. Summoned to the headmistress's study, to see her alone on some trivial matter, a great sexual gust blew through him, which he did not in the least understand. He makes it clear that no physical contact took place between him and the grave middle-aged lady. "I desired nothing of her, as she desired nothing of me: that no word was spoken by her, and no gesture made by her, which even within my present experience I could have imagined to be remotely sexual." The experience was "terribly sweet and poignant . . . and at first with no touch of shame in it. I thought it unique, this 'feeling' as I called it: something I had been specially chosen for, something granted to me and to no one else." [9] He prayed for its return and thus began a half-innocent autoerotic life. "I can't remember clearly when a change took place, and I began to have feelings of shame and guilt; but I rather think that it was at puberty, and that terror at the sight of my first small emission (which occurred just as I was waking from sleep) was the occasion for it. I remember that terror very clearly indeed. I thought, with a sudden appalling stab of apprehension, that I was desperately ill, and that masturbation was the cause of whatever complaint I was suffering from. I had no idea at all of what this might be: I just thought of it vaguely as something terrible. Shortly afterwards my father came up to my bedroom one morning while I was still in bed, and stood looking out of the window, half turned away from me, in great embarrassment. After a minute or two he was able to say, 'There's nothing to worry about in what's happened to you: it's nature': then tried to say something else, failed and left me. My terror was over, but self-accusation remained: and in respect, not only of masturbation, but of my day-dreams and their subject matter too." [10]

These experiences could be mirrored in many childhoods. In *Friendship-Love in Adolescence* [11] a Russian psychologist studied the sex and love life of a Russian schoolboy as recorded in his letters, diaries and recollections and those of his friends. When the boy, John, was just over fourteen years, "A large number of 'country cousins' were staying on a visit with John's people. John slept on the floor in a certain room. In the morning when he awoke he found something wet and sticky was on his underclothing. The thought came to him that his father (who used to get up very early and take his breakfast in his room) had spilled some jam on him . . . when carrying jam for (or after) his breakfast through the room in which John was sleeping. . . . The adult John has a considerable number of recollections concerning his pollutions. . . . He remembers that they would take place during a voluptuous dream." [12] The dream concerned bathing women he spied on from the cliffs around Odessa. Like Gollancz he feared some disease. He could not speak of the pollutions to his parents. He associated them with things bad, sinful or illicit. But the whole point of this study is that he was going through a series of intense love-friendships with other boys and that these were presently to give way (in his fifteenth year) to love-friendships with girls. Life at this dimension was not only rich and meaningful, but totally unsexual and unconnected by him with the awakening of the sexual. The sexual was simply a nuisance. There is a letter, earlier than this event, showing him with a Gollancz expertise setting about the organization of a dark-room in a strange house so that he could continue his passion for photography. To sex a stranger still, in his photography he is as confident and skilled as an adult.

The technological and dynamic passions of the latent child have behind them the emotive crises of infancy, and we may suppose if it helps us a generalized relation to infantile sexuality. The Oedipal conflict involves a sublimation. But it is impossible to see latency purely in Freudian terms but rather as a biological or primatial necessity which delays full sexual power until the physical powers and technical skills which enable the creature to handle the familial consequences of sexuality have been acquired. It is a misfortune that we see everything through Freud's sexual eyes, in terms, that is, of sexual success or failure, and forget Adler's will-to-power— forget too the vast human realm of the cerebral, the intellectual, the creative, the scientific in which the pulse of sex beats faintly or not at all. Why, in that world, as we have seen, even sex itself becomes a subject for objective, unemotive investigation, almost a matter of pure theory as though it no more existed within the investigator than galactic forces. The rediscovery of the centrality of sex in life, which we owe to this century, easily makes us overlook the intellectual, technological and social structures from which it has been dismissed and to which the growing child is introduced *as if they were all that mattered.*

There may be a psychosocial blunder here. But the fact is there, "a fact-of-life" in contemporary culture, and it has to be reckoned with in understanding the role of sex in society.

CHAPTER *nine*

THE PRIVATIZATION OF
HUMAN LIFE

1

It is important to remind ourselves what childhood is actually like from the time when the avid mammalian infancy is over
and locomotor and sphincter control is achieved. Gone are the
milky breasts, the soft bosoms, the everlasting bottles, the instant
meals, the changed diapers, the intimate cleaning, the powdering of
cracks and crevices which made the child's helpless body an extension of the mother's rather than a proud independent possession.
After infancy the movement is toward increasing individuality and
privacy and to a stubborn opposition to being dominated or restricted. Progressively, dressing, washing, bathing, urinating and
defecating pass into the *child's* control (by a similar progression
he comes to the table to eat in a family meal rather than is visited
to be fed).

With his autonomy grows the possibility of his silence. Central
to his social and intellectual growth is his command of speech. At
first he is talked to, then he repeats talk, then he talks back. Pres-

119

ently he talks to himself, at first out loud, then noiselessly. The interior comment he makes begins the structuring of his interior space where he belongs to himself in privacy and no one else can follow. The life of the interior space, carrying with it the power to achieve an exterior silence, is the real precondition of his autonomy. Through the cogitations which take place within his interior space he learns how to manage and to deceive others. To protect his own privacy and autonomy he may be forced to lie as to whether he has washed, or moved his bowels, that morning. The concealment preserves his freedom of action, his right to regulate his life at his own pace. He presents not his inner self in answer to every demand made upon him but what he chooses to reveal and in the light that he chooses. This is the structuring of the mask by which he will henceforth live and behind which his real self will grow. Childish untruthfulness is usually measured by its effect on those at the receiving end rather than its role in the protection of the independence of the child. A friend of mine had a little girl who was fond of sitting up in bed and cutting out patterns in colored paper. One day her mother found cuts in the counterpane. "Margaret, did you cut the counterpane with your scissors?" her mother asked. "No, Mummy." "Well, you do like cutting out paper patterns, so you could have done it, couldn't you?" "No, Mummy." "Well, Margaret, God sees all you do." "Yes, but he doesn't tell you all he sees." It was the perfect example of consciousness of an interior space which could not be invaded even by a loving parent. And God too had a right to his silences.

Even in primitive societies many bodily functions are exercised in private. One recalls the Australian aborigine woman, whose whole life was nakedness, saying that it made her ashamed to be caught in intercourse by the children. For this she and her man always went apart, screened by bushes and windbreaks. From the standpoint of most primitive societies the Western obsession with privacy must look both neurotic and expensive. Western society more and more secures to its members the private bed or bedroom. A child may even be able to exclude his siblings from his room. And the bathroom with the lock inside is socially obligatory. Certain acts must be performed in the completest secrecy. The logic of the smallest room is that the whole world except the user can be excluded from it. Floods of shame and guilt overwhelm the child who fails to limit the proper function to the proper room, or who soils anything with his excrement. He must try to conceal (or deny) even the wind he breaks.

The topography of the modern house or flat is an indication of the cultural values attached to bodily privacy, not simply over affairs of the toilet, but over the separation of the sexes from each other, of parents from children beyond the Oedipal stage, and of guests from all. Long gone are the days when the tutor or usher shared the bed with his pupils, or, as in New Testament times (and down the centuries too), the whole family slept together in one bed,[1] or Poil de Carotte shrank from the prickly hairiness of the uncle whose bed he shared on a visit, saying, "Uncle, you know I love you very much but I can't go to sleep if your hairs prickle me."

The dismissal of excretory functions to places behind locked doors is part of the whole cultural drive to make the body and its acts private. The body is placed at a distance, is accepted only in the degree that it is groomed and inoffensive. Desmond Morris is correct in his assumption that man is a naked ape who is *conscious* of his nakedness. The incident most revelatory of the whole Judeo-Christian cultural tradition we have inherited is that in Genesis, where Adam speaks to the Lord God: "I heard thy voice in the garden, and I was afraid, because I was naked; and I hid myself." The reply of the Lord God is the voice of contemporary thought, "Who told thee that thou wast naked?"[2]

The distancing of the body takes place in speech forms too; socially inacceptable bodily functions are referred to indirectly or by euphemism—"business," "No. 2," "wee-wee." The child at school, announcing his bodily needs to a master, distances them through the polite formula, "Please, sir, may I leave the room?"

The more private the bodily parts the more difficult it becomes to refer directly to them in social or familial intercourse. The mere mention of them in speech becomes a kind of unveiling. There is a corresponding self-consciousness about the words for sexual organs. The acceptable and proper (dictionary) words are still felt as too clinical and scientific, the Anglo-Saxon equivalents, the famous four-letter words of the literary debate, as too gross and active, too emotionally compelling, to be acceptable. The screw of inhibition was even tighter in Victorian times. Mrs. Theresa La Chard, brought up strictly in the seventies under a father who "insisted that one should never mention any part of one's body between chin and ankle," was forced to give her stomach the fantastic name "ankle-chin." [3] Victorians were excessive in their prudery, clothing even the legs of tables, and our society is infinitely more free. But it too sets up barriers which must not be broken in normal intercourse. The fact that a literary avant-garde breaks them in novels and plays does not mean that they are therefore broken by society. It is many years since Eliza Doolittle said, "Not bloody likely" on the stage and the public was shocked (and delighted). But the epithet "bloody" is still not generally acceptable in conversation in British society, and can invite reproof.

The psychological clothing is a mirror of actual clothing. The naked ape has become the clothed man. It is one of the most significant of the cultural achievements which separate him from his animal forebears. Of course, it had its primary justification in utility. Clothing took the place of fur as the conserver of bodily heat and protection from powerful sunlight. But peoples who go almost naked still adorn themselves. Their clothing is of the minimal cultural sort which proclaims status or office or intention and frequently provides a symbolic sexual privacy. For people so little privatized in life and body a total nakedness—the loss of belt and penis sheath, say—still gives them the same feelings of shame and exposure that nakedness would to us. Therefore one has to see clothing in the same way that we see private rooms, or the interior silence I have spoken about, as part of the necessary *privatization* of individual lives, the *sine qua non* of the human condition. And over clothing, with us from shortly after birth, and taken down with us into the grave, a different sort of consciousness must pervade us from an animal consciousness. There cannot be any sense in which an animal can be naked or clothed. For man there is the either/or. For civilized men the clothed condition is the normal, the social one, required even by law, and not just convention, if nakedness involves exposure of the sexual organs. "Clothed and in his right mind" is the accepted scriptural cliché for a man going about his business in the world. His person begins with his clothing. He is under no compulsion, accident or illness apart, ever to reveal his nakedness to anyone; rather the contrary, it is only on special occasions that nakedness is either privately or publicly acceptable. The consequence is that not only are others shut off from knowledge of his body, but *it is hidden from him.*

Our externals, our clothed front against the world, become part of our human dignity, or the mask of the persona we present to others. As soon as choice of dress becomes possible, we decide in what seemliness we shall be seen by others and transfer to the clothes themselves the sex appeal or nonappeal of our naked bodies, devising our own signals in place of natural ones. So much do clothes become part of us that any stripping of the body under compulsion is felt by the child as a gross indignity, by the adult as an invasion of the personality, and any hostile stripping as destructive of it, and intentionally so.

In 1552 the Portugese galleon *São Jodo* was wrecked on the coast of Natal. Under their commander, Manoel de Sousa, the crew and slaves and noble company began a forced march through savage and hostile country. Finally, the party was broken up and Manoel de Sousa and his wife, Dona Leonor, and children and a small group were robbed and stripped by hostile Kaffirs. The record continues:

Here they say that Dona Leonor would not let herself be stripped, but defended herself with buffets and blows, for she was of a nature to prefer being killed by the Kaffirs to being left naked before all the people. There is no doubt, even, but that her life would have been over if Manoel de Sousa had not begged her to let herself be stripped, reminding her that all were born naked, and, as it was God's will, she should not now refuse to be so, too. One of their great trials was seeing those two little children of theirs there crying and asking for food whilst they, the parents, were unable to help them. When Dona Leonor was left without clothes, she flung herself to the ground immediately and covered herself completely with her hair, which was very long. She made a hole in the sand in which she buried herself up to the waist and never arose from it again. Manoel de Sousa then turned to an old nurse of hers who had been left with a torn shawl and asked her for it to cover Dona Leonor with, and she gave it to him. For all that,

Dona Leonor never again consented to arise from the spot on which she had flung herself down when she had been left naked. . . . When the men who were still in their company saw Manoel de Sousa and his wife naked they moved away a little, being ashamed to see their captain and Dona Leonor so. Then she said to André Vaz the pilot: "You see the state we are in and that we cannot go on any further and that we must end our lives here, for our sins. Go on your way, save yourselves, and commend us to God. If you reach India or Portugal at some future time, tell them how you left Manoel de Sousa and myself and our children." [4]

We are manifestly in the presence of a universal cultural phenomenon. Summarily put, nakedness is concealed as civilization advances—man moves the consciousness of his visible self from his body to his clothes. This is the process of privatization which begins with the mind and is properly, necessarily, extended to the body as the object and concern of the mind's private life. I would surmise that this is an irreversible cultural process belonging not just to the moral sphere but to the heightened sense of the sovereign and independent person proper to higher civilization.

2

But if this privatization is understood as necessary to one's human standing and unselfconscious functioning among one's fellows (Carlyle had a point, in *Sartor Resartus,* about the manner in which human assemblies would be reduced to absurdity by nakedness), one's proprietorship of one's own nakedness has to extend to respect for the privatization of the nakedness of others. Some consequences follow. One's own nakedness, though concealed from oneself, though placed at a distance from consciousness, is never lost; it remains a concern, an anxiety of the mind, something continuously known, though less familiar than the clothed self. On the other hand the nakedness of others simply disappears from our consciousness. As for some of those we are familiar with, we cannot conceive their nakedness and find it hard to make the effort. The more we respect and value them, the more disconcerting it is to try; the mind rises in revolt and blocks the exercise as an offense against propriety, a mental assault upon them. This is true of parents in their relations with their own children when their children's bodies have passed the point where they are washed and cared for as an extension of the parental body. But it is *most* true of children themselves. They are born and grow to speech and understanding in a totally clothed world (in which their own nakedness may be for a long time the only nakedness they ever meet) and they must conceive of and come to understand other human beings as clothed beings. As they themselves come to understand the indignity and deprivation of forced nakedness, so they revolt against any mental stripping of parents and other loved and respected and admired ones. Clothed being is the real being-in-the-world for others. The only *unclothed* being of others is the face. In it their outwardly turned being is concentrated. The child grows up signaling to and being signaled by other faces, interpreting and being interpreted by them. In the presence of the powerful face-to-face world the unseen body becomes even more negligible. Could not children nevertheless grow interested in the nakedness of those with whom there is no emotional or familial tie? This they do. The small schoolboy at Odessa became a voyeur, he spied from the Odessa cliffs on unknown women bathing below him but not on his mother or sisters, which would have been inconceivable. The sex play of children is often a mutual discovery of nakedness under the clothes and exploratory as much as sexual. Through the nakedness of those who do not arouse an emotional response the child learns indirectly, and approaches obliquely and delicately, the nakedness of those dear to it.

In an important interview in *The Times*,[5] Dr. Louise Eickhoff, a psychiatrist, condemned sex education in schools as (contrary to the general opinion) the cause of psychical disorder in children. Among the things she said were, "Sex education interferes with the parental bond." "The psychiatrist has long known the disruption of sexual teaching or experience received in the anal-erotic phase (eight to nine years) of development. True, children pass stories round, but it is quite different with your contemporaries—you can always tell them to shut-up," and "I am now treating four 10-year-olds, two boys and two girls, who would never have become psychiatric cases if they had not received sex instruction. Recalling their teacher's words, they actually vomit."

It seems to me that what Dr. Eickhoff is speaking of in a psychiatric context is precisely the cultural phenomenon I am describing, that the acceptance of one's own privatization is bound up with the incapacity, *even mentally,* to invade the privacy of most others. The child to whom human coitus is described has instantly to relate it to the behavior of his parents, whose nakedness has been totally dismissed, and to whom the functions hidden by clothes are unknown. He is now invited to a total invasion of the privacy of his parents, a psychical unveiling, which is also his own unveiling. For some it is psychologically impossible to accomplish the unveiling, it only invites illness, the mental balance is disturbed because the canons which have hitherto governed life and never hitherto been questioned are suddenly thrown away, and a totally new perspective is demanded, irrespective of the degree of emotional maturity of the child.

This can be illustrated from life. The following story comes from my childhood autobiography, *The Living Hedge.*[6] It needs a brief explanation. My friend and I, both about eighteen, were idealistic members of a youth movement which had adopted a "chela" system. The full member was supposed to win and train and foster a young recruit who would ultimately enter the older movement.

Looking back I see that we were both ignorant and naïve, more in need of instruction than able to teach. But we readily thought of ourselves as *gurus* and proudly sought out *chelas* and after many arguments over bad cups of coffee in the cafés of Peckham and New Cross decided that our first duty to them was elementary instruction in sex to counteract the "filthy" view it was certain they would otherwise pick up. My candid and shell-pink chela took my revelations—nervously transmitted through a protective screen of tobacco smoke—very calmly. Indeed, with a touch of indignation, for the thought that his voice might presently break (something he had never previously considered) shocked him into the realization that he would have to leave his church choir and he would lose the seven shillings and sixpence a quarter paid to him. An alternative source of income would be a paper round at thought of which he shuddered. He said *it was not fair* that his voice should presently break and often returned to the subject with surprising bitterness in the weeks that followed.

My friend Roly's educational talk with his chela had a more disconcerting outcome. He interviewed his chela "in the drawingroom where we sang Victorian ballads together on Sunday night and the little boy sat on the kind of horse-hair chair that pricked one's bare knees, amid the vases of pampas grass and the china presents from the seaside which climbed above the mantelpiece in a squirrel-run of tiny platforms and posts and pillars of polished mahogany. I wondered afterwards how he got rid of Granny, who, partially deaf and almost completely blind, used to wander in and out of that room continually and disorganize by her very presence any serious conversation. If you said to her that you wanted to be private that was the surest way to induce her to shuffle around after you and gossip.

"Roly's chela was a neurotic child at the best of times and far from phlegmatic. Under Roly's owlish instruction he became hysterical and would not let him finish.

"He pulled ornamental plates off the sideboard and hurled them at Roly. 'It's not true, it's not true,' he shouted. 'You're just lying.' He dashed the chair he was sitting on to the floor and kicked at it in his rage.

" 'Liar! Liar;' he shouted. 'My mother would never do a thing like that.'

"Roly, alarmed at the whirlwind he was reaping, approached him with the gentleness that was instinctive to him in the presence of the unenlightened.

" 'But . . .' said Roly. 'Have *sense*.'

" 'Don't you come near me,' shouted the boy, now beside himself with anger and grief, 'or I'll stick this knife into you!' And he drew from his stocking the skene dhu which had been Roly's present to him.

"He pushed the table between Roly and himself and ran out of the room, shouting insults. And whenever afterwards he met Roly in the street he crossed scowling to the other side as if Roly were a monster whose presence contaminated the air. . . ."

3

Psychologists have noted that when a child is intentionally, and with kindness, allowed to view the nakedness of his parents, after having made his own psychophysical withdrawal into privacy he may suffer shock and subsequent disturbance of the same order as accompanied Dr. Eickhoff's little patients. The previously unknown naked adult body is quite unlike his (or her) own body and even menacing in its shapes and sexual signals. It has been remarked that the human child is more *unlike* the human adult than the offspring of any other primate is like its parents; it is more like the member of another species. Children are not little adults as baby monkeys are little monkeys. Empathic identification is not therefore so easy. Dr. Desmond Morris has remarked that man may have the largest brain but he also has the largest penis of the primates. The gross sex signals of female breasts and buttocks and male penis are something totally unexpected in the child who has not grown up in their visual presence.

Margaret Mead has explained [7] that there is a world of difference between Western culture and the culture with sufficient nudity to permit the child to observe in his siblings, in the adolescents and adults of his village, the stages by which he will reach manhood or she, womanhood. His elder brother is a boy like himself, who counts himself a boy and plays with boys, but obviously he begins too to be a man like his father or his uncle; the quite small girl, though far from being a woman, is already budding breasts. In a society in which the transitions are not visually presented, the little boy has no means of knowing how he may become that which his nude father is, and so can be alienated from what he sees.

This century is one which has at last opened a door on nudity in the cult of the beach. On the beach a high degree of nakedness is permitted; total nakedness only for very tiny children, as yet. Here it is possible for a boy or girl to observe in a beach throng some of the most important physical transitions to manhood and womanhood. But valuable as it is, we are compelled to recognize that it is a highly controlled and aesthetic nudity which is produced. The genitalia and the female breasts are concealed, if minimally.

The ideal of the beach cult is the beautiful bronzed body of young athletes—a Grecian conception indeed. By the standards of the cult anything *else* is uncalled for. The withered, shapeless bodies of the old in their nudity are an affront, a psychological offense, and the old know it. Not all nudity is pretty.[8]

Any further advance in nudity would require a change of the law, for it would become indecent exposure, and a change of law so far-reaching in its implications and so far not taken by any civilized society, would produce a national moral and psychological crisis. Semi-nudity is accepted in sport, in camping, and nudity accepted in family bathing parties. It has reached the theater, though it always had some acceptance there. We are less inhibited than the Victorians. But the special, brief periods of exposure (for how long can the ordinary individual keep his beach culture going?) only emphasize the value the culture places upon the privatizing of the body. What is permissible (or practical) on the beach is unacceptable in hotel or boardinghouse or school; what is worn for work is seldom worn for holiday too. Social restrictions have been relaxed, but not abandoned.

In the same degree that consciousness of the body is moved from the skin to the clothed exterior, the sexual signals are displaced. Dress now proclaims the sex, even perhaps from infancy on, and in most civilizations is the first and most obvious visible distinction between sexes. So innate is it to most cultures that to dress in the clothes of the opposite sex constitutes an offense, a form of misrepresentation; it is equally an offense to gain admission to a place (a public lavatory for instance) reserved for the opposite sex. Of course the elements of aggression in sexual signals have to be transferred to the clothes too, hence all the glitter and sophistications of male and female attire in highly complex societies. The language of attire may simultaneously signal not only sexual invitations or refusals but age, role, status, pecking order in society. We are soon back again in the Quant-Laver world of the clothes of sexual aggression and display which in other animals is the prerogative of the animal body alone. But clothes which offer invitations like flashing neon signs are still privatizing, not only of the body but of the intentions of the wearer. They are selective in their range, reaching only those for whom they have this appeal. They

pass over the heads of those for whom the appeal has no meaning
—children, the old, servants, members of another culture. And as
Mary Quant almost remarks in that interview to which I have often
referred, sexual clothes have a deep ambiguity, they cover and defend that which they are also intending to display. For that reason,
the clothed or half-clothed body has more sexual allure than the
naked one. With the naked body, the mystery is at an end; with the
clothed one, even the minimally clothed one, the torment and appeal of what is at once disclosed and not disclosed is always there,
the question of what is intended by the clothed sexual display is
always raised, stimulating the imagination. The sexual ambiguity
of clothing reflects not only the ambiguity of the role of the sexual
in society itself but also the longing for sexual mystery.

The significance of clothing in the latency period is plain enough.
It reinforces all that makes for privatization and simplifies the
release of the child into the challenging world of the nonsexual.
And what latency actually means in a highly sex-conscious society
two stories illustrate. I was walking down Charing Cross Road
when the Cameo-Royal Cinema was featuring an avant-garde film.
Over the entrance of the cinema had been erected an enormous
blown-up photograph showing an actress, whose name I have forgotten, naked on a platter of fruit and vegetables. Vulgar-comic
really. Next door to the cinema was the Golden Egg restaurant, its
title and a chaste ovoid picked out exquisitely in indirect golden
lighting. Approaching me were a small boy and his mother. He
was staring across the street, I thought, to where I was staring too.
His eyes danced and he pulled excitedly at his mother's arm. "Oh
Mummy," he said, "look at the Golden Egg!"

The second story concerns an exhibition of French art. I was
walking alone in a salon of glorious nudes. The walls were blazing
with Boucher-like girls sprawling fondant-rosy and virginal on
clouds of divinely blue silk. A small French boy and his parents
came abruptly into the room. The boy gave a cry of pleasure and
broke into a run. *"Oh maman,"* he cried, *"regarde les petits ois-
eaux!"* There was a center table, which I had missed, covered with
tiny, exquisite porcelain figures of birds and animals.

CHAPTER ten

THE DISTANCING

OF THE BODY

1

Lady Bennerley, a Jane Austen character who strayed into *Lady Chatterley's Lover*,[1] remarked, "So long as you can forget your body you are happy—And the moment you begin to be aware of your body, you are wretched. So, if civilization is any good, it has to help us to forget our bodies, and then time passes happily without our knowing it."

It was clever of Lawrence (who did not believe a word of it and who fought all his life for an electric body-consciousness) to have got this sentiment down on paper. The paradox reveals the ambivalence of our relationships with our own bodies and those of others. We are our bodies and, paradoxically, our bodies are our instruments. As instruments of our wills, our bodies and their organs have to possess a transparency in order to be effective. The eyes could not "see" the outer world if they "saw" themselves. The eyes, to be instrumental, must be withdrawn from the field of vision. For the hand to be effective in grasping, manipulating, moving objects we have to be conscious, not of the hand, *but of what we are doing*. The learner-cyclist falls off his cycle once he becomes self-conscious about his limbs. He becomes expert when his feet and hands are the transparent conduits of his intentions. The ballplayer simply would not develop skills if he were conscious all the time of the exertions of his body in meeting the demands of the game. At another level the body performs a host of actions which sustain it the more vigorously the more they are sealed in unconsciousness—the beating of the heart, the circulation of the blood, the digestion of food, the maintenance of body temperature. When these processes obtrude into the consciousness then it is usually because something has gone wrong with them.[2] This relationship with our bodies is so fundamental that we never, in normal life, give thought to it at all. We just as unconsciously exploit it. The tools and instruments we contrive are artificial extensions of our limbs and senses and we use them just as transparently as we use our bodies, looking *through* the microscope at the forms revealed on the slide, reaching *with* the walking stick to poke the pig. We even see, in a more total way, the complaints of the body brushed aside, its agonies swept into the subconscious, in crises in the work of a scientist, an explorer, a worker in a civil disaster, a soldier who continues fighting after being wounded, who does not even notice that he is wounded.

The body is not to be defined as a *substance* in the world, something rounded off and completed, apart from a few minor adjustments in time and/or a mechanical process of aging or wearing out. The body is an activity in the world about which it can be said that what the activity is accomplishing is often more important (to us) than the instrumentality by which it is accomplished. The digging, the hoeing, the raking in the garden, are only the means to the flowering end.

We note the good sense of Lady Bennerley's remark. The self-effacement of the body equals happiness; persistent bodily consciousness equals misery. We can transpose the point into the argument about privatization made in the last chapter. The process of privatization assists that effacement of the body which the persistence of *activity in the world* seems to demand. We are made clumsy as instruments by too intense a bodily self-consciousness. The link with the latency period is immediately plain, for this is when technical mastery is accomplished. The child discovers what he can do in the world and how he can do it. Over against infancy and adolescence, childhood is a period of diminished bodily self-consciousness. Perhaps this is not precise enough a statement—the infant lives *in* his body, the adolescent lives *aware* of his body. In both growth phases bodily *presence* is crucial. In latency the bodily presence is muted or distanced in favor of movement, exploration of things, mastery of the muscular self and of the world. It hardly needs saying again that this is the dimension of the nonsexual, or the asexual in childhood. I have pointed to the relationship between this phase and the tasks the child, when become man, must face in the world—the economic, political, social, or even military roles he must ultimately play. It looks as though this realm of technical mastery demands the same muting of sex, the same disembodiment, as the latency period. Put another way, it is as though the values of the latency period have taken over a whole dimension of human life. The objectivity of latency has come more and more to dominate the life of adult man while the subjectivity of infancy and adolescence has diminished as the criterion by which life should be lived. This is the way the cultural pattern appears to be developing at a phenomenal rate.

The latency phase is dominated by play. Erikson felicitously analyzes the fence-whitewashing episode in *Tom Sawyer* to demonstrate the element of fantasy in play. The young victim, Ben Rogers, comes across Tom whitewashing the yard fence. "Ben's gait was the hop-skip-jump—proof enough that his heart was light and his anticipations high. He was eating an apple, and giving a long melodious whoop, at intervals, followed by a deep-toned ding-dong-dong, ding-dong-dong, for he was personating a steamboat. As he drew near, he slackened speed, took the middle of the street, leaned far over to starboard and rounded to ponderously and with laborious pomp and circumstance—for he was personating the *Big Missouri*, and considered himself to be drawing nine feet of water. He was boat, and captain and engine-bells combined. . . ."

And this witnesses to the childish need to act out fantasy in play.

But not all fantasies are generous and lighthearted and not all play, or all fantasy realized in play, is so innocent and gay. The novel *Quarry* [3] by Jane White tells of three teen-age boys who capture and hold prisoner a younger boy and use him as the vehicle for their fantasies and lusts and as a surrogate for their inadequacies, finally wreaking vengeance on him by murder for the innocence and gaiety they have lost and envy. Robert Musil's *Young Törless* or even the classic *Tom Brown's Schooldays* reveal the ease with which play and fantasy move over into sex sadism. There is an element in the play even of young children which disturbs the adult—destructiveness for its own sake, sadistic experiments on animals, insects or other children, delight in the exercise of power, and a detached, impersonal curiosity just to see "what happens" when something is set in motion. We may speak of it as an element of coldness in play: the powers of the player are being discovered and exploited; it is almost a *sine qua non* that consequences should not deter it. But if we believe that the whole realm of the technological, the industrial, the commercial, the political, the military in contemporary society is *especially* the translation into adult life of the impersonal mastery impulses of latency, we must expect magnified there not only the freedom, objectivity and daring of the child's exploration of his world but also the ruthlessness, coldness, insensitivity which can characterize it too. Indeed when we reflect upon the new technological world we have entered, which threatens to overwhelm and dehumanize us with its grown-up mechanical toys, and about which so many prophets have warned us, it is as if we had strayed by accident into the world of the monstrous child prodigy, capable of any mechanical and cerebral feat, but incapable of being swept through and through by mercy, pity, love. Incapable, in fact of being adult.

2

I have spoken of this world not only as a nonsexual world, but as a disembodied one. It is striking indeed how much of our life contrives to be disembodied. Social anthropologists have made much play with speeded-up crowd films which show the extraordinary skill with which hundreds of people will mill around in a confined space and against all probability avoid physical contact. It is the case that the major part of adult life—in factory, school, shop, university, home—is carried on with the minimum of physical contact. The socially permissible public contacts are rigidly formalized—the pat, the handshake, the elbow grip, the kiss. Between individual bodies a dimension of gesture and language intervenes. To assert the right of access to other bodies is an act of defiance of the social consensus. To sum it up in an epigram, man loses his body in his activity.

What happens *then?* Man has put his sex and the sex of others at a distance. "We are commonly dressed, and commonly behave as if we had no genitalia," William Golding wrote.[4] Man has lost, and has sought to lose, his body in his mobility. He has expanded the objective, technological interests of latency into the dominant motive of a whole culture to which the sexual is irrelevant, from which it is excluded except as a salable product like boots or jam or as a field of unemotive investigation like astrophysics. It is culturally a phenomenal achievement and one product of it is the technologically mighty Western civilization. But it is not so much the civilizing of sex as the desexing of civilization. This was in Freud's mind when he spoke of the monstrous superego of contemporary civilization. For at the end of the day man is still Desmond Morris's naked ape, he still has his body and his genitalia. He not only lives with his body, but he is his body; he not only has his genitalia but they cry out for satisfaction. It is not surprising that sex is the great casualty of contemporary civilization. Perhaps we may put it a better way: In the struggle between sex and power the casualty rate is inevitably high; people are destroyed in their sex and their humanity by the conflict.

Yet to speak of the cultural process as sheer loss would be nonsense, not to say ingratitude to the long struggle of man to hold securely to his sex and to his society, to have a life which, however hard the discipline, *contains* them both. There is a sense in which his sexual life is heightened by the civilizing process, which intensifies sexual consciousness and experience of the erotic not only by the displacement of sex from erotic zones to the clothes but by the diffusion of sex into the art and literature and music of civilization, into the décor and ethos of a culture, into the groundswell of social intercourse. That which is officially disciplined surges up into the symbolism and gestures of a society like the murmur of a mutiny at a parade. Primitive societies take time off from discipline in permitted orgies. Civilized societies subvert the discipline, in the name of other values, as we saw Mary Quant doing as one representative figure of a teen-age culture which self-consciously challenges the gray elderly people it imagines totally devoted to sexual suppression.

Yet it is not the contemporary sexual mutiny alone which concerns us but also the profound contribution of privatization to the erotic life. The privatization is of course not just physical (clothes, disembodiment) but psychological (shame, modesty, secret desire). The erotic breaks through the barriers created by disembodiment and privatization. It lays bare the hidden hungers, the concealed wonder; it acknowledges them and feeds them. Privately, in the relation between persons, it encourages and provokes the passion for interpersonal exploration, an exploration which is a genuine revelation of the being of the loved-other and of oneself. It shocks the individual into self-discovery and the discovery of others, into the knowledge of what we are behind the public disembodiment and the privatized face. It was perhaps for this reason that Marguerite Yourcenar made the Emperor Hadrian say (in *Memoirs of Hadrian*), "I have sometimes thought of constructing a system of human knowledge which would be based on eroticism, a theory of contact wherein the mysterious value of each being is to offer us just that point of perspective which another world affords. In such a philosophy pleasure would be a more complete but also more specialized form of approach to the Other, one more technique for getting to know what is not ourselves"; [5] and, we might add, the "getting to know" ourselves too in endless discovery and rediscovery, and in a privatization which has become dual, not singular.

3

D. H. Lawrence is still the prophet of this erotic understanding and its spiritual value. There is a moment of shock in *Lady Chatterley's Lover* almost without equal in contemporary literature and quite without the unease which accompanies those exhaustive lyrical-ecstatic descriptions of copulation between Connie Chatterley and gamekeeper Mellors—written it would seem as a duty. It is the moment when Connie has failed to get an answer at the front door and innocently walks into Mellors' backyard:

So she went round the side of the house. At the back of the cottage the land rose steeply so that the back yard was sunken and enclosed by a low stone wall. She turned the corner of the house and stopped. In the little yard two paces beyond her, the man was washing himself, utterly unaware. He was naked to the hips, his velveteen breeches slipping down over his slender loins. And his white slim back was curved over a big bowl of soapy water, in which he ducked his head, shaking his head with a queer, quick little motion, lifting his slender white arms and pressing the soapy water from his ears, quick, subtle as a weasel playing with water, and utterly alone. Connie backed round the corner of the house, and hurried away to the wood. In spite of herself, she had had a shock. After all, merely a man washing himself; commonplace enough, Heaven knows!

Yet in some curious way it was a visionary experience: it had hit her in the middle of the body. She saw the clumsy breeches slipping down over the pure, delicate, white loins, the bones showing a little, and the sense of aloneness, of a creature purely alone, overwhelmed her. Perfect, white, solitary nudity of a creature that lives alone, and inwardly alone. And beyond that, a certain beauty of a pure creature. Not the stuff of beauty, not even the body of beauty, but a lambency, the warm, white flame of a single life, revealing itself in contours that one might touch: a body!

Connie had received the shock of vision in her womb, and she knew it; it lay inside her. But with her mind she was inclined to ridicule. A man washing himself in a back yard! No doubt with evil-smelling yellow soap!—She was rather annoyed; why should she be made to stumble on these vulgar privacies.[6]

That is superb for its realism as well as its sense of revelation. It brings us back to the question I asked earlier—What happens *then?*—which I raised about privatization and disembodiment. If we look at what happens in society we may fairly speak of a flight from the body, a flight into the world, as the human condition. In *The Naked Ape* Desmond Morris paints a convincing picture of the primitive pair bond—the male off into the bush in the morning, member of his cooperative hunting group, and returning in the evening to the family hearth with his share of the spoils of the chase. The female left behind, nurturing the children, guarding the hearth, muting her sexual signals lest the pair bond be endangered by luring other males. He drew a comparison with the male commuter and the housewife of the contemporary society. The flight of the male is a physical movement away into a realm of activity which demands total concentration, disembodiment, as the price of success. The female's life, though more static, is a hardly less total immersion in tasks and duties. But there is always the home-coming:

> Home is the sailor, home from the sea,
> And the hunter home from the hill.[7]

For the hunter it was a genuine physical return to tribal camp, to the safety and total social life of the warm herd, to his woman and children gathered together in his own bed from their tasks and play, like the New Testament father of whom I spoke. The reward is renewal and restoration. Male and female recover from their exhausting tasks, they relax free from tension and danger, they are warmed by the rediscovery of belonging to the tribe, and each other, by the plunge back into family and social roots. It is the universal human return as night falls, a preparation for the healing and forgetting sleep brings, itself a physical rejection of the demands and strains of the objective world. Metaphysically, it is a return to the stillness, darkness and safety of the womb. We can speak of it as a reembodiment. The body is re-entered, the flesh rediscovered, the erotic becomes paramount, that which was only fantasy in daytime moments of leisure now becomes fact. Two become of one flesh. We have stumbled on a fundamental human rhythm—the daytime disembodiment under the demands of the world, the night-time rejection of the world in sleep and sex. It is relevant to this insight that during sexual intercourse the messages of sight and hearing are subordinated to, or obliterated by, tactile sensation, that primitive, universal "feeling" which is distributed throughout the body. We can witness this return in children too, in their latency especially. Boy and girl, they leave play and companions and return home. And in a moment, their lives can become softer, gentler. Even the little boy, fresh from his raucous masculine assertiveness, wearied and emptied by its imperious demands, will rest his face in his mother's lap or on his father's shoulder, to reassure himself of his belonging, his security in the midst of the family.

What I have been describing is both a rhythm and a tension. The tension is between the demands of the world and of the body; the rhythm is the necessary movement from one to the other. The tension heightens the life in both; the rhythm permits the reversal of roles and so enables the tension to be lived without destruction. From such an analysis we reach a view not only of men and women as complementary, but of their sexual relations as a source of healing or re-creation—of reconciliation especially with the fact of "embodiment." We reach Lawrence's view of sex as redemptive in individual lives as well as the source of new life. We can understand his denunciations of the Midlands society he knew as a boy as barren and gray because (as he believed) it failed to enjoy (or rejected the enjoyment of) sex as the redemptive, fulfilling, creative core of human life. But once we ask *why* that society, or any other society, fails to enjoy or rejects the enjoyment of sex in such a sense, we are lost again in the social and psychological thickets from which we had just hopefully emerged.

CHAPTER eleven

"INTER FAECES ET URINAM NASCIMUR"

1

The antithesis is not only between day and night, work and rest, the world and the body, but between the human spirit and the conditions of life. Man is not *satisfied* with the conditions of human existence. History shows an almost permanent rebellion against them. Even the most primitive of peoples buried their dead. They found it impossible to leave the bodies of loved ones to the jackals, the vultures, the ants. To see them rent to pieces was to be rent internally. It was hard to believe in the total extinction of those with whom one's life was so completely identified. Quite early man showed himself unable or unwilling to accept the fact of death as an inevitable part of human existence. It might be said that in the doctrine of immortality man *elected* to live beyond the grave. His rebellion has taken many forms—complaint to his maker, hope in a Redeemer, the scientific dream of world mastery, the contemporary myth of human perfectibility through revolution. He has raged not only against sickness and death but against natural disaster, poverty, war, inequality, injustice, sin. He has waged the war of the spirit against the world in which he lives, a war which Camus described as "the persistence in that hopeless encounter between human questioning and the silence of the universe."

In the course of that questioning he has turned his rage against his own body. I do not only mean by such acts as mutilation, flagellation, castration or ascetic practices directed voluntarily against his own body, but also by his will to reject the body as the vehicle of his existence and to live apart from it.

The *Vishnu Purana* [1] speaks eloquently of human affliction in terms which match the complaints of Job.

When the child is about to be born, its face is besmeared by excrement, urine, blood, mucus, and semen; its attachment to the uterus is ruptured by the Prajapati wind; it is turned head downwards and violently expelled from the womb by the powerful and painful winds of parturition; and the infant, losing for a time all sensation when brought in contact with the external air, is immediately deprived of its intellectual knowledge. Then born, the child is tortured in every limb, as if pierced with thorns or cut to pieces with a saw, and falls from its fetid lodgment as from a sore, like a crawling thing upon the earth. Unable to feed itself, unable to turn itself, it is dependent on the will of others for being bathed and nourished. Laid upon a dirty bed, it is bitten by insects and mosquitoes and has not power to drive them away. Many are the pangs attending birth and many are those which succeed to birth; and many are the afflictions that are inflicted by elemental and super-human powers in the state of childhood covered by the gloom of ignorance; and internally bewildered, man knows not whence he is, who he is, whither he goeth nor what is his nature; by what bonds he is bound; what is cause and what is not cause; what is to be done and what is to be left undone; what is to be said and what is to be kept silent; what is righeousness and what is iniquity; in what it consists or how; what is right, what is wrong; what is virtue, what is vice.

From birth pangs the *Vishnu Purana* leaps immediately to the infirmities of old age, sparing nothing; then the teacher says, "I will now describe to you the agonies of death."

The human self-discovery of such passages in religious literature is equaled by Leonardo da Vinci's protest in his *Notebooks*. There, meditating on the continual death and renewal of the body, he exclaims that nature is so fecund that "she is more ready and swift in creating than time is in destroying; and therefore she has ordained that many animals shall serve as food for one another. . . . Our life is made by the death of others. Men and animals are really the passage and conduit of food, the sepulchre of animals and resting place of the dead, making life out of the death of others (taking pleasure in the misery of others), making themselves a covering for corruption." [2] The *Vishnu Purana* describes the child as born from a sewer; Leonardo defines the sewer.

2

The rage against the body is most easily turned into rage against human sexuality, for many reasons. The first is the tyranny of sex. A man may more easily master other appetites than he may master the sexual. He can come to terms with his greed, repress or sublimate his aggression, humble his pride. But his sexual appetite leaps up unawares, to take possession of him, to fill him with desire, with lust, which in his mind he would gladly be rid of, if not permanently then at many of the inconvenient moments at which it takes over his body and consciousness, and still more, with shame and despair at the forbidden or unattainable other persons toward whom his appetite, perhaps unexpectedly, is directed. This is peculiarly the experience of adolescence; latency has not taught the child toward whom or what his appetite may be so terribly directed. It is in the sexual experience that every man discovers his animal state: he is ridden by forces he does not understand. But if virility is not always open to suppression, potency equally is not always his to command. Sexual power may assert itself when it is not wanted, and vanish when it is. Sexual power can be, in relation to a man's total social life, many times an impertinence or a humiliation. It would be a delusion to suppose that this is a situation man ever could (or given the centrality of sex would ever want to) bring to an end. The price of his most exalted experiences is to put up with the discomfiture of never being totally his own master, but of being frequently his own monster. There is no utopian wood-with-windblown-anemones waiting for our sexuality to discover, no Lawrentian sexual utopia into which we can retreat, closing the gate on the world.

It does seem the moment to remark that to many women the physiological element in marriage is a distasteful one, to which they submit, *faute de mieux* or by *force majeure,* for the sake of what is more richly valued—love, children, the home, status, fulfillment. William Golding speaks of this with profound understanding in *Free Fall.* With a boy's angry passion Sammy lays siege to the beautiful Beatrice and wins her. But it is not only her loveliness, but her calm and inviolability which torment him. He wants to break that down and reach the interior being from which, he argues accusingly, she keeps him out. She loves him, she has been *brought* to love him, and so she submits to intercourse, not only from love, but from fear of losing all that their love has begun to promise. But her submission is with a clenched fist and aching head, as if, records Sammy, to a T.A.B. injection. "What had been love on my part, passionate and reverent, what was to be a triumphant sharing, a fusion, the penetration of a secret, raising of my life to the enigmatic and holy level of hers became a desperate shoddy and cruel attempt to force a response from her somehow. Step by step we descended the path of sexual exploitation until the projected sharing had become an infliction." [3] Only years later, long after that desertion which destroyed her, did he come to recognize the beauty of her simplicity as Dante recognized that of his Beatrice. The negative personality he had seduced, he now saw to have been full and glowing. "She was simple and loving and generous and humble; qualities which have no political importance and do not commonly bring their owners much success."

Golding there—indeed throughout *Free Fall*—tragically illuminates the qualitative differences between male and female sexuality. It is the more important now to recognize this difference and to see what obligations it places upon society because we live in a time when male sexual imperialism blurs the difference in the male interest and turns the female into a junior male, that is a person with the same tempo of sexual life as the male, except that she must accept male arousal and domination.[4]

Richard Hettlinger, in his acute analysis of student sexuality,[5] has much to say of this. After noting that Kinsey had brought to light the fact that men reach the peak of their sexual energy in the late teens whereas women reach it only in the late twenties or early thirties, he said, "There is, therefore, absolutely no reason for the young man to assume that because *he* wants to pet to orgasm or engage in intercourse, his girl—even if she is madly in love with him—is either interested in or attracted by the prospect."

Hettlinger goes on: [6]

The second qualification noted by Kinsey is the fact that women are far less aroused by psychological stimuli to sexual excitement than men are. The average male is readily excited by the thought of coitus; and as soon as a relationship becomes at all intimate, he tends to think in these terms, thus compounding the pressure toward sexual fulfilment. But the average girl, certainly if she is sexually inexperienced, is likely neither to engage in fantasies of coitus nor to be stimulated erotically by such thoughts. Kinsey made a careful and interesting study of thirty-three kinds of erotic psychological stimulation by which the majority of men are affected. These included nude pictures, the genitalia of the other sex, burlesque and floor shows, animals and humans in coitus, erotic stories, lavatory drawings, and discussions about sex. He discovered that the majority of women were largely uninterested in and unaroused by such things. The only items that produced comparable interest among women were motion pictures (not specifically pornographic) and "literary materials" (i.e., novels, essays, and poetry). And in both these instances, as Kinsey noted, it may well be the romantic element, rather than the explicitly sexual content, which appeals to the woman. But in any case it is obvious that factors leading to intense sexual stimulation in the man may leave his partner cold.

Hettlinger pursues this argument, making very strongly the point that Kinsey tends all the time to identify *"sexual* arousal with *genital* arousal" and that this confusion brings him to the unexamined conclusion that "for women as well as for men, sex is focussed in, and primarily fulfilled through, the physical pleasure of genital orgasm." William Golding's Beatrice is the classic literary example of the young man's expectation that the girl he desires will be a mirror image of himself. Yet where the physical diffidence Beatrice shows is not present, where the woman fiercely desires, with nymphomaniac intensity, penetration, possession, by the male, there may go along with it that resentment of male sexual imperialism of which, as in so many other things, D. H. Lawrence is the interpreter. He is writing of one of those illicit encounters between Connie and Mellors:

And this time the sharp ecstasy of her own passion did not overcome her; she lay with her hands inert on his striving body, and do what she might, her spirit seemed to look on from the top of her head, and the butting of his haunches seemed ridiculous to her, and the sort of anxiety of his penis to come to its little evacuating crisis seemed farcical. Yes, this was love, this ridiculous bouncing of the buttocks, and the wilting of the poor, insignificant, moist little penis. This was the divine love! After all, the moderns[7] were right when they felt contempt for the performance; for it was a performance.[8]

Presently, Lawrence is explaining an equally valid *male* rage, of Mellors against luckless Bertha, his wife.

"She had to work the thing herself, grind her own coffee. And it came back on her like a raving necessity, she had to let herself go, and tear, tear, tear, as if she had no sensation in her except in the top of her beak. The very outside top tip, that rubbed and tore. That's how old whores used to be, so men used to say. It was a low kind of self-will in her, a raving sort of self-will: like in a woman who drinks. Well in the end I couldn't stand it. We slept apart."[9]

3

What we have been speaking about so far is sexual conflict purely in the realm of normality. If we consider abnormalities, perversions, fetishisms, then the sense of possession by powers we do not understand and cannot finally master becomes tragically obvious. The homosexual does not understand his/her condition or how he or she came to acquire it. It is not often that he or she can change it, or that physicians can do so. However much he or she may desire normality, marriage, children and home may be closed to him/her forever. Not by willing or praying or fasting is his/her sexual orientation likely to change direction and fasten itself on a legitimate love object. The flagellant, the sadist, the masochist, the fetichist, the pederast, each is caught in a sexual trap. His sexual satisfaction is outside his will, and maybe outside his moral code, "fixated" on an object or erotic pattern of behavior beyond that which society can tolerate. Normality in sexual life at least promises a socially useful and personally fulfilling end even to sexual activity regarded with contempt. Perverse and fetichistic activity is as useless, as unrewarded, as it is compulsive.

Krafft-Ebing [10] records many cases where a quite fortuitous association of some extraneous event with sexual excitement leaves an "imprint" on the sexual life which it is almost impossible to escape from. In case 47 he discusses evidence taken from Feré's *L'Instinct Sexuel*. B, a small boy, was about to masturbate with another boy at the corner of a street, where the gradient was steep, when a heavily laden dray, drawn by four horses, came along. The driver was yelling at the horses and whipping them. The horses slipped and struggled on the cobbles and the sparks flew. "This excited B very much and he ejaculated as one of the horses fell." And ever afterward similar scenes would have the same effect and he would go in search of them. He was trapped for life in a certain sexual pattern.

In case 103, he reports an example of fetichistic entrapment. X, the son of a general, raised in the country, was initiated at the age of fourteen "into the pleasure of love by a young lady. The young lady was a blonde, and wore her hair in ringlets. In order to avoid detection in sexual intercourse with her young lover, she always wore her usual clothing—gaiters, a corset, and a silk dress on such occasions." For the rest of his life similar conditions had to be fulfilled or he could not enjoy intercourse. "He was always compelled to give up thoughts of matrimony, because he knew he would be unable to fulfil his marital duty in night clothes."

One has to assume that the cases of B and X came to be recorded because at some point the patients sought medical advice. But what of the many cases unrecorded, "lived with" in secrecy, because they could be "managed" or secretly gratified—the world of Gillian Freeman's *Undergrowth of Literature?* And what disasters can occur, even in families which believe themselves enlightened and articulate about sex, but are unaware of their secret exploitation of it, is brought home by the case of Mark.

Mark, a pubertal thirteen-year-old boy, was referred for psychiatric evaluation by his parents with complaints of frequent and violent temper tantrums, aggressive sex play with two younger sisters, open masturbation in the presence of others, and of having made a number of direct sexual propositions to his mother. During the intake interview the parents attributed Mark's difficulty to "heredity," and described the countless ways in which they had demonstrated their love for him. His mother had first explained the sexual facts of life to him in great anatomical detail when he was four years old, and had continued the didactic portion of his education with regular refresher courses. They did not want him to grow up believing that sex was dirty and shameful, which was also their expressed reason for regularly having sexual intercourse in his presence.

He had suffered severe night terrors since an early age, and at these times his parents readily accepted him into their bed. In order to "comfort him" he would be permitted to sleep between them. As these nightly visits increased in frequency, Mark's father found himself becoming irritated and uncomfortable because of "overcrowding." He solved this problem by moving to Mark's bed. This arrangement became standard during the several years preceding reference.

Upon examination it was apparent that Mark suffered a severe, chronic psychotic illness, and immediate confinement was recommended. Because there would be an unavoidable waiting period before admission would be possible, the caseworker tactfully suggested to the parents that they have Mark sleep alone in his own bed. The father, who had already described himself as a well-trained and thoroughly-read "student of child psychology," demurred on the grounds that "the boy might interpret this as a rejection." [11]

Kinsey, and common sense, to say nothing of the vast literature of sexuality accumulated in this century, warn us that it is never easy to separate normal from perverse sexuality. The possibility of perversion is present in "normal" sexual lives. People, long after puberty, can be sexually corrupted. Myra Hindley became Ian

Brady's devoted and silent assistant. Gilles de Rais never lacked lieutenants and huntsmen in his campaign of sexual murder. The Nazi extermination camps flowered with perverts in jackboots. Lust feeds where it can and the attraction of positive evil in sex, of sexual power over others, is far older even than Petronius's *Satyricon*. In our own society it is all that is understood by sexual criminality.

4

We have to recognize the presence of sexual horror in sophisticated societies. It is less surprising than it might be after what has been said. What is this horror? One can analyze it psychologically or psychoanalytically and speak of it as the product of sexual anxiety. This does not dispose of the anxiety, still less of the horror: mankind is probably more not less sexually anxious since the absorption of the Oedipus complex into Western culture than before, or so the growing numbers of the mentally ill might attest. It is inescapably the case that sexual fear and anxiety are part of man's quarrel with his human condition, which I analyzed in *Alternatives to Christian Belief*. I spoke there in particular of Camus's rebellion against a universe which produced so much needless suffering of the innocent, suffering which is often, or even principally, sexual suffering. At the same time we have to comprehend man's shrinking from his own body, not simply from his powerful and would-be autonomous genitalia, but from his interior organs, from his frightening vulnerability to injury, disease, death.[12] So man protests his body, and especially his sexual condition, and this is basic to his self-civilizing struggle, to his self-making in a cultural, religious and intellectual sense and cannot be reduced to the consequence of an infantile trauma unless we evaluate that trauma symbolically as the earliest point in his struggle for self-mastery, even against the body.

The sexual horror expresses itself aesthetically, just as the erotic does. In *Doctor Glas*,[13] Hjalmar Söderberg spoke the nineteenth-century romantic disenchantment: "Even today I've hardly recovered from my astonishment. Why must the life of our species be preserved and our longing stilled by means of an organ we use several times a day as a drain for impurities; why couldn't it be done by means of some act composed of dignity and beauty as well as of the highest voluptuousness? An action which could be carried out in church, before the eyes of all, just as well as in darkness and solitude? Or in a temple of roses, in the eyes of the sun, to the chanting of choirs and a dance of wedding guests?"

St. Augustine put it brutally: *"Inter faeces et urinam nascimur."* Other Christian fathers, struggling with paganism, were as fierce. For St. Bernard man was "nothing else than fetid sperm, a sack of dung, the food of worms." If man for St. Bernard was "a vile dunghill," woman, for Tertullian, was "the gate of hell." Marcion argued that the world was "stupid and bad, crawling with vermin, a miserable hole, an object of scorn." It was impossible to think of God as the author of "the disgusting paraphernalia of reproduction and for all the nauseating defilements of the human flesh from birth to final putrescence."

It is not necessary to go on listing the "antisex" pronouncements of so many Christian authorities. They are endlessly rehearsed by sex reformers as evidence of a perverted Christian view argued by them to persist down to this day. I do not cite them as evidence of some special Christian aberration, but as sharp examples of man's sexual protest—a necessary episode in his struggle for self-mastery.

5

That struggle gives birth to another dimension of man's sexual life, so far unvalued, but which alters all other sexual and human values. I mean the experience of love. The struggle for self-mastery is the struggle for self-regard. But that entails *other-*regard. One great civilizing force in Western civilization has been the slow climb of women out of slavery and chatteldom—out of the role of childbearer and lust slaker ("better to marry than to burn")—to an equality in terms of personality with man. It has brought in its wake, with unprecedented force, the vast wave of romantic love.[14] And while, biologically speaking, membership of the human race means theoretically that any male can have coitus with any female, the concept of romantic love insists, *only this man with this woman.* At the height of its power to bind two loving beings, love means that sexual relations outside the pair bond are, though not impossible, held to be degrading and destructive. Certain forms of sexual activity within the pair bond even may be felt to have the same consequences. Sexual relations must instead serve and heighten love rather than replace it. When the mutual passion is at its zenith it is felt as a commitment to union "till death do us part" and the idea of a contract to love for a few years and then to find new partners would be as psychologically unbearable as promiscuity. In the passionate love bond two persons feel of one spirit as well as one flesh.

What I am speaking of is an ideal, perhaps even a dying ideal in the general cynicism overtaking Western society, but it is an ideal which has generated a tremendous dynamic and we have only to turn back to what Mary Quant spoke of in the interview discussed in the opening pages to see the impact of passionate love on the unprepared young. She speaks of girls as well prepared for the physiological side of sex by instruction in schools but overwhelmed by the unexpected impact of romantic love. If it is true that the best and highest love humanity knows involves the condition *only this man with this woman,* then we have an additional motive for fear or anxiety about sex. For coitus outside the bond, into which one may fall without ever "intending" to, defiles the bond; the "body" may betray that which the "spirit" knows is its highest good. It is a universal experience. What it all implies is the sacralization of sexual activity by fullest personal love. The problem for the sex reformer who wants sexual freedom is how to get it without throwing away all that love between two faithful persons brings to the enrichment of their own lives and of civilization itself. The standard of romantic love makes casualities of persons who cannot sustain it or achieve it. The efforts to do away with it in the hope of sparing the casualties might bring disaster on the whole culture instead.

CHAPTER *twelve*

SEX IN A DISINTEGRATING CULTURE

1

We have been examining sex as an element in a culture and as the disturber of a culture. The human sexual dimension is not subject just to psychological and biological conditioning but to cultural determinants. Indeed the biological and psychological assessments of sex are themselves part of a larger cultural assessment. They are never independent. It has been remarked that Freud's Oedipean sexual psychology is only fully realized in the professional, Jewish middle-class family in central Europe in the late nineteenth century in which the father was authoritarian or tyrannical and the gender roles sharply distinguished. The anthropologists have found it inapplicable to many primitive societies and the sociologists might find it unreal in the tribal life of a San Francisco hippy pad. Indeed, it loses much of its force in the small family situation in the West today where the father shares more and more the intimate rearing of the baby and so becomes himself a stand-in "mother" whose function gives rise to a mutual emotional dependence of the kind from which Oedipus excluded him. And in any case the Oedipean psychology is a *male* psychology. It was only with difficulty that an Electran female counterpart was built up; it has never played the shattering role of Oedipus in the modern consciousness. But Western culture is no longer exclusively male in the nineteenth-century sense, and a sexual ambivalence of the sort which would have been incomprehensible then has now become acceptable to our society. It is marked by clothes and hair styles. It could be the first-generation response to a non-Oedipean situation—one in which the child ambiguously identifies with the sexuality of both parents and jealousy is sibling-directed rather than father-directed.

Be that as it may, in a technological society in rapid social change, in which the area of activity where sexuality is irrelevant is enlarged every decade, the sexual life is bound to pass through crises dictated by the need for personal satisfaction and sexual status on the one hand and for social stability on the other. Social stability would seem to demand a strong pair bond and an affectionate, private family life in which children can grow up in emotional security. It also would seem to demand clear gender roles —the more adult gender roles become confused, the more difficult it is for children to recognize their gender and to come to sexual maturity. Of course, gender and sociosexual roles are codified in Western law and what we are witnessing is a cultural drift in the face of the law, a drift which expresses itself in opposition to the law and to demands for its reform in the direction of a general permissiveness. Divorce law reform, abortion law reform, the removal of adult male homosexuality in private from the stigma of criminality, the drift from the toleration of contraception to its recommendation—these are landmarks familiar to everyone. They go along with important cultural changes—the bikini cult, the miniskirt cult, greater awareness and toleration of sexual deviations, greater freedom of discussion and publication of sexual material, and that increase in sexual promiscuity among young people which is everywhere talked of but not very precisely known. In all this, society would seem to be fulfilling in the sixties and seventies the program of such avant-garde societies as the Federation of Progressive Societies and Individuals of the thirties of which the famous Professor Joad was leader. Its program had a double orientation—toward freedom and toward healing. The doctrine of freedom was based on the argument that men and women were entitled to be treated as adults in matters of sex, and not to be deprived of knowledge or information about techniques or insulted by oppressive sexual laws coming down from less civilized times. It was a theory of man's sexual coming-of-age. The complementary doctrine of healing was that society was sexually sick with a puritanical sexual hangover and would be healed only by bringing all that festered in darkness into the light, a cleansing of the Augean stables for which freedom was indispensable. "Morality is strengthened by liberty." The whole radical and progressive movement in the thirties was inspired by utopian and idealistic dreams. Man and society could be made better; human perfectibility was not quite out of reach. The prophets were H. G. Wells, Bernard Shaw, Bertrand Russell, Karl Marx and Lenin. To move mankind on, it was first necessary to reverse the processes of Victorian society. If the Victorians had kept sexuality under iron taboos but allowed free reign to capitalist acquisitiveness, the new society would free sex from its chains but put wealth and exploitation under clamps.

Yet apart from the logical perversity of this standpoint, it simply is not the case that sexual liberty and sexual healing are identical aims. Their presence in the same revolutionary manifesto simply confuses the issue. Sexual healing presupposes a concept of sexual health, a norm toward which the best efforts of a culture may be directed. Sexual liberty can only mean liberty for the deviant as well as for the "healthy": the concept of a norm is inconvenient to it. The real conflict is not between sexual freedom and sexual oppression but between concepts of sexual health and sexual liberty.

Of course, law, custom, morality in the West presuppose a sexual norm. Sexual rights are legalized within the marriage bond; outside it no sexual acts have any obligatory nature and no one has a claim to the sexuality of another. Laws do not necessarily punish adultery, but adulterous persons do not have claims on each other unless children are born. Homosexual relations, and other sexual deviations condemned by custom and morality, have been usually punishable at law, as have prostitution and the sexual exploitation of children. The legal point of view is the immemorial Christian view that sexuality is not morally or socially acceptable outside the marriage bond.

This is not the norm the sexual reformers have cared for; for them it disguised the sexual sickness of society. The evidence of novelist and psychoanalyst combined to reveal the sickness. Both personal and social ills were traced to the traumas of sexual growth and development, and the all-too-often thwarted search for fulfillment. In the wake of Freud, D. H. Lawrence made himself peculiarly the prophet of sexual healing and suffered martyrdom of a sort for it. It was a spiritual disaster for him to have his search for sweetness and candor in sex confused in the police mind with pornographic exploitation of sex. "Sex does not exist," he wrote,[1] "there is only sexuality. And sexuality is merely a greedy, blind self-seeking. Self-seeking is the real motive of sexuality. And therefore, since the thing sought is the same, the self, the mode of seeking is not very important. Heterosexual, homosexual, narcissistic, normal or incest, it is all the same thing. It is just sexuality, not sex. It is one of the universal forms of self-seeking. Every man, every woman, just seeks his own self, her own self, in the sexual experience. . . ."

And what he felt about the sacredness of sex came out strongly in his polemic *Pornography and Obscenity:*

Pornography is the attempt to insult sex, to do dirt on it. This is unpardonable. Take the very lowest instance, the picture postcard sold underhand, by the underworld, in most cities. What I have seen of them have been of an ugliness to make you cry. The insult to the human body, the insult to a vital human relationship! Ugly and cheap they make the human nudity, ugly and degraded they make the sexual act . . . I am sure no other civilization, not even the Roman, has shown such a vast proportion of ignominious and degraded nudity, and ugly, squalid dirty sex.[2]

Sex, he argued, had been driven into the underworld and he himself would be quite prepared to censor pornography rigorously. These were brave statements, and *Lady Chatterley's Lover* spells out his reformist attempt. He proclaimed that the act of intercourse itself was a spiritual as well as a physical union. When it was an act of full and flowing mutuality it transformed the partners. They were made over by its beauty; for this fulfillment they existed. But a deliberate effort had to be made to cleanse sex of "the accumulated lingual filth of civilization." Not only was it proper to describe coitus as graphically as any other physical occurrence might be described, but the four-letter Anglo-Saxon words could be redeemed from obscenity and brought back into literary and polite discourse again. The result is a novel of much wild beauty allied to a suffocating didacticism. Richard Hoggart was perfectly correct in asserting at the trial of *Lady Chatterley's Lover* that Lawrence belonged to the English puritan tradition and that his novel witnessed to the protest of his conscience over the treatment of sex by society. Dr. John Robinson was surely right, too, in arguing that Lawrence saw the act of intercourse as something as sacred as holy communion. But Lawrence could not succeed in his bid for the sacralizing of sex—he could not succeed psychologically within his novels, I mean, to say nothing of succeeding within society—because he was hostile not only to the degradation, but to the civilizing of sex. Despite his tirades against a greedy, individualistic sexuality, sex in its lyrical perfection in his works is something separated from society, it is the adding of the flame of a man to the flame of a woman (or the flame of a man to the flame of another man), the coming together of gods and goddesses in their private empyrean, and he has nothing but scorn for *society* when it lays hands on these private and necessary raptures.[3]

His novelistic program of sacralization is only possible because he cheats on the sociology of the situation, at least in *Lady Chatterley's Lover*. Mellors is married to a drab and a scold, Connie to an impotent but possessive invalid for whom she can never be more than nurse and companion. There are no children to Connie. Moreover Sir Clifford Chatterley is an improbable trinity of everything Lawrence most hated—the successful but shallow writer, the cold landed aristocrat, the ruthless coal owner. He is meant to verge on the monstrous [4] and his emasculation symbolizes the England Lawrence despaired of. The real test, not of the private mysticism but of the social worthiness of the erotic exploration by Connie and Mellors of each other, would rest in more normal circumstances. Suppose Sir Clifford Chatterley were not impotent, suppose Mrs. Mellors were ordinary, if unloved, suppose there were children on both sides? Then the Connie-plus-Mellors fertility theme would look rather silly: the didactic theme collapses, and of course even the most hated societies do not lack fertility. Which leads to the question, if coitus is to be sacralized, how is it to be contained by society, how is it also to be civilized? It is not simply the sex act in itself which rests constantly in need of this but the whole dimension of sex in any society—and peculiarly in our own pluralistic society. Surprisingly enough it was the trial of *Lady Chatterley's Lover* which brought this sharply home, posing, in a manner which would have horrified Lawrence most of all, the choice between healing and liberty.

2

The prosecution of *Lady Chatterley's Lover* in 1960 was advanced under the Obscene Publications Act of 1959 which, Lord Birkett said,[5] placed the law of obscenity on a more modern and more sensible footing. It made possible a trial by jury of the publisher of any work which had been the subject of a prosecution and the calling of witnesses for both defense and prosecution. The earlier act, the Obscene Publications Act of 1857, had permitted a "search and destroy" operation of anything judged pornographic or obscene by a magistrate. When Miss Radclyffe Hall's *The Well of Loneliness* was condemned under this act neither she nor her publisher was allowed to give evidence; they had no standing in a misdemeanor at common law. There is no doubting the good intentions of the new law and Lord Birkett spoke of it in glowing terms. "It has set up what I hope will prove to be a real protection for literature. Our literature running back through the centuries is one of our very richest possessions and chiefest joys. To protect the writers of today and tomorrow in the full and free expression of their thoughts by the safeguards contained in the new act will prove of immense benefit as the years pass and tastes and opinions change. . . . It is no little satisfaction that the writers of the future may breathe an ampler air." [6]

C. H. Rolph, commenting a little sourly on literary censorship in the *Kenyon Review*,[7] drew attention to a remark of Pierce Hannah in *The Times* (in the course of a review of *The Other Victorians,* by Steven Marcus) to the effect that the Victorians swept pornography under the carpet while we give it the most comfortable chair in the house. "We, no less than the Victorians have our current cant. Ours is to protest that books and plays with only the most tenuous claims to be taken seriously must be fought for because they contain once taboo words and situations . . . we make martyrs out of the third-rate writers in no danger of going to the stake."

Rolph drew attention, too, to the remarks of Mr. Gerald Gardiner, Q.C. (now Lord Gardiner), at the end of the trial to the effect that no one should imagine that because Lawrence used four-letter words in his particular way in his particular book, they can be used by any scribbler writing any sort of novel.

"But it has seemed to follow," Rolph remarks. "The four-letter scribblers have come into their own. The lavatory wall has lost its unique function.[8] The Obscene Publications Act, 1959, was essentially the work of a Society of Authors' Committee of which the chairman was Sir Alan Herbert and I was the secretary. It had fourteen members. Five of them to my knowledge have since doubted that, in the event, the cause of English literature was furthered by this act of 'liberation.' "

He was not one who doubted, but he saw the point that since 1960 "the stuff by cartloads comes in," and the healing evangelism of Lawrence has foundered in a general permissiveness. As this is much to the point of my whole argument, it is necessary to look at the direction taken by the post-Old Bailey literary movement. It is a cultural phenomenon of high importance. The point does not turn around the debate on censorship or on definitions of pornography but on the direction taken by the culture as a whole. One has to ask whether this amounts to the decivilizing of sex.

3

One begins, unfortunately, with the moral world turned up-side down of the Marquis de Sade. In *Juliette* he wrote: *"Le mal est nécessaire à l'organisation vicieuse de ce triste univers. Dieu est très vindicatif, méchant, injuste. Les suites du mal sont éternel-les; c'est dans le mal qu'il a créé le monde, c'est par le mal qu'il le soutient; c'est pour le mal qu'il le perpetue; c'est imprégnée de mal que la créature doit exister; c'est dans le sein du mal qu'elle retourne après son existence."*

In *Justine* he speaks in more atheistic and determinist terms. M. de Bressac tells Sophie that the God she believes in is the fruit of ignorance. If all that happens is the consequence of natural laws by which Nature herself is enchained, then what becomes of God, what role has he, and what point is there, he asks, in moral re-sistance to natural facts? In *Juliette* he spells this out in sexual terms: "The strong individual, when he despoils the weak—when, that is to say, he actively enters into the enjoyment of those rights Nature has conferred on him, and exercises them to the full—reaps pleasure in proportion to the extent to which he realizes his poten-tialities. The more atrocious the harm he inflicts upon the helpless, the greater will be the quiverings of voluptuous delight which he will feel. . . ." [9]

From male sexual imperialism de Sade moves in a smooth transi-tion to a natural justification of murder. Again it is M. de Bressac philosophizing to Sophie. "Two hideous actions confront your un-philosophic eyes: the destruction of a creature like to ourselves, and the augmentation of the evil arising from the fact that this creature happens to be my mother. As far as the destruction of one's kind is concerned, you may be certain, Sophie, that such a belief is entirely chimerical, since the power of destruction has not been accorded to man. At the very most he has the ability of causing things to change form—but he cannot annihilate them. Moreover all forms are equal in the eyes of nature; and nothing is lost in the immense crucible wherein her variations are achieved." [10]

It is the kind of didacticism de Sade plugs laboriously in every pornographic work of his. Everything man does is justified because this is the way nature made man.

And what this base philosophy wraps up is an endless series of debauches—the destructive sexual invasions of the weak in the power of the strong. If it all began with *Les 120 Journées de Sodome* which de Sade wrote in prison, then its origin is in an obsessive and uncontrollable masturbation fantasy. "The [imagined] orgies, too, involve every kind of cruelty, torture, and violent death, till the pages drip with semen and blood," Alan Walton says. In order to get erection and orgasm in his solitariness, de Sade whips his imagination into even more cold, despairing and violent episodes.

The translator, Alan Walton, defends the enormities on three counts, that de Sade anticipates many of the insights of psychoanalysis, that the things he describes actually took place in the vile century he lived in, that de Sade was doing about sex what Voltaire did about the world in *Candide*. The last is quite untrue: the humorless de Sade is no satirist. Voltaire was not recommending the follies he exposed, but flaying them. De Sade commends the follies as the true way of life. As to the first point, one acknowledges the half-insights of de Sade, but to place him on all fours with Freud is to dishonor Freud—one has to imagine Freud approving the murder of the father and the impregnation of the mother by the Oedipal infant! It is true that many of the deeds de Sade celebrates were drawn from actual ones. But then Krafft-Ebing as obviously described actual cases without coloring, exploiting or recommending them. To describe orgiastic sexuality in the hope of understanding and curing it is far different from relating it in the longing that others will adopt satyriasis as a way of life.

The point that such deeds took place is an important one, though. Is that to be a final judgment on their desirability? One argument surely made in the preceding chapters is the infinite variation in human sexuality, the human sexual restlessness in fantasy and fact, the capacity of the sexual drive to escape personal control on the one side and on the other the need to contain and civilize sex if society and its values are to be sustained. A substantial part of human history concerns the socialization of sex in this sense. But as sex does not just "disappear" under disapproval, but gets suppressed or sublimated, the tension remains and the unexpected or unwanted triumph of sex over civilization or humanity or morals is an endless story. It is to this tension that we owe the existence of a sexual subculture in every civilized society. We have such a subculture in a personal sense—everyone has two sexual lives, one of intermittent actual experience, the other of continuous fantasy. The life of fantasy is exploited in a thousand ways in society—in our times by a commercial subculture of pulp magazines, sexy advertising, *Playboy* and its like, strip-tease shows, art magazines, blue movies, highbrow sensationalism, realistic television, and so on endlessly. It can even be summarized by *Playboy* bunny clubs, where the rule is, do not touch, do not date, which is an invitation to feed the private fires of fantasy. Fantasy would appear to be the price paid for disciplining sex impulses, but it has a positive side in the heightening of the sense of the erotic in life, the deepening of romantic love, the birth of sexual idealism; it is more than a series of imagined erotic scenes, it is also the dialogue of the soul about sex, morality, love. But the test for a society is whether it can contain its erotic imagination and prevent the issue of the sex of the imagination into cruel and destructive deeds. It is the special role of de Sade that he is the spokesman of the subculture. He wants freedom for sex to operate without moral and social controls. He wants the subculture to become the dominant culture. One of the things that has happened is that the 1960 Old Bailey decision over *Lady Chatterley's Lover* has released the de Sade stream into English literature and extinguished the Lawrentian stream.

An expression of Lawrence's singles out the central element in the indictment of de Sade. He was angry with those who wanted to "do dirt" on sex. He stood for its sacralization. De Sade stood for its defilement. Every character who passes through the pages of his works defiles, or is defiled. No one ever loves, no one ever *lives* outside the categories of lust, murder, or theft. It was once said that the nihilist is a disappointed idealist. The sexual defiler is the disappointed sexual idealist; he does "dirt" on sex out of his rage. What he can never recover from is that Gilles de Rais actually existed and worked his will as he pleased on the shepherd boys his posses hunted down in the hills.

Of course, de Sade was not alone. He was really the founder of the *roman noir,* of the whole movement Mario Praz celebrated in *The Romantic Agony.*[11] If that movement expressed a longing, it was surely for license for sexual activity no matter how perverted, without let or hindrance, for the overthrow of the contemporary culture of restraint; it was a movement which took seriously Chateaubriand's words: *"Je fus toujours vertueux sans plaisir; j'eusse été criminel sans remords."* Edmund Wilson spoke of the movement founded by de Sade as "a literary tradition of erotic cruelty, hysterical enjoyment of horror and perverse admiration of crime." The deliberateness of its break with the European tradition, with the moral consensus of Christendom, in the interests of a criminally organized society is beyond dispute. I think it is not to be denied that it is this stream of literary consciousness which has followed *Lady Chatterley's Lover* into the open. But first we must identify it.

4

David Storey's *Radcliffe* appeared in 1963. It was his third novel. *This Sporting Life* and *Flight into Camden* were works of power as well as promise. Storey himself relives in his novels the divisions in his own life—he has been a professional footballer in a mining village and an artist at the Slade School. In *Radcliffe* he is probably both his heroes, the burly Tolson, the sensitive Radcliffe. It is impossible to describe *Radcliffe* simply except to say that it is the *Wuthering Heights* of this century—as deeply romantic, as passionate and exalted in language, and with an absolutely destructive love at its core. The decaying mansion of a dying aristocratic family is also central to the book. So are the dreary town closing ever more relentlessly in and the grim moors of an immemorial England across which archetypal figures stride through stars and storms and sunsets of a Jungian intensity. It is a mad, blazing book with scenes painted in the apocalyptic violence of one who is still in his bones a painter. Along that dimension *Radcliffe* marks a return of the poetic imagination, of poetic symbolism, to the novel, as remarkable as in *The Centaur*.

Leonard Radcliffe is the last child of a once rich and aristocratic family. Handsome, sensitive, melancholy, there is something pathological in his withdrawal from his family even as a child. The only person with whom he can connect as a boy is a big domineering schoolboy, Victor Tolson. Tolson resents it when his slight, princely friend wins a scholarship to a better school and fells him with a secret assassin blow which puts the younger boy in hospital. When they meet again in manhood—Tolson married with two children, Radcliffe incapable of normal social relations—the same violence is to characterize their renewed homosexual love affair. It is told in Heathcliffian terms of passionate pursuit and bitter resentment; a tension is built up which can only end in murder. It is the most horrible murder in fiction since the murder of Nancy by Bill Sykes. Radcliffe destroys Tolson by repeated blows on the skull with a hammer. (It is almost a precise anticipation of the homosexual murder of the young Edward Evans by Ian Brady, which led to the cracking of the Moors murders case.) We are spared nothing in the description. All the heightened poetic symbolism of the book spins it into a passage capable of making one physically ill. Storey here has no idea of his power. He is still a writer afraid of not having enough.

There are other passages of an equal obscenity. Tolson and Radcliffe work for contractors who put up the canvas cities of county shows—and take them, and their latrines, down again. After a great agricultural show they dispose of the innumerable vats of human excrement by emptying them across the sloping meadow. The stench of this episode pervades the whole book; it is symbolic of the mad obscenity of human life. The second passage to which I must draw attention is a description, of clinical precision, of a most appalling rape—Tolson rapes Radcliffe in the mouth.

Radcliffe first conceals his crime of murder, then confesses, then is confined for madness. What follows is degeneration and death. A psychopath has killed a moron and just about everything alive at the beginning of the book is dead at the end. But there is an attempt at a philosophical justification of it all. The story is held to be symbolic of the "histrionic schizophrenia" from which Europe is suffering. "The battle was so intense between us because we could see something beyond it. It was the split between us that tormented us; the split in the whole of Western society." Radcliffe follows this in court with a platonic justification of homosexuality as a "power that creates order" in society. He argues that it was an impersonal relation, almost a communal relation, he sought with Tolson.

Counsel asks:

"But don't you feel that you're obscuring something which is personal by giving it this cloak of objectivity, by theorising? . . . you are so aware of what occurred that you can only overcome your sense of distaste and guilt by explaining it in terms of the general corruption of society?"

"No, No, it was the other way around!"

"Why then did you *kill* him?"

"Because I had to! . . . Whatever we did we destroyed. Everybody! Everything!"

"What does that mean?"

Leonard had turned away. He seemed senseless. "Oh, God!" he cried, shaking his fists at the court. "I wanted something huge and *absolute!* I wanted an absolute! I wanted an ideal! I wanted an order for things!" [12]

This is the kind of heartfelt cry to the God-shaped blank that Jimmy Porter might have made.

Of course we have to recognize that this is the author speaking, not Radcliffe. For him, the struggle between a brute and a sensitive man sums up the European dichotomy, but not once in the story, apart from the statements in court, do we really recognize in Radcliffe a search for some great human ideal, some redemption for all men. What Radcliffe seeks is compensation for his own timidity and weakness. In a Krafft-Ebing case-history fashion he seeks a sadist to satisfy his masochism. It is the author who wraps something else around it.

I have dealt with *Radcliffe* in some detail because it represents a watershed. The literary freedom the acquittal of *Lady Chatterley's Lover* conferred on the serious writer is exploited with gusto and relish to the point of obscenity, and with more than a touch of genius. But the author straddles the divide. He is not exploiting his own lust through characters who are projections of his perversities, but looking with an effort of compassion on people caught as he believes in the deadly sexual and spiritual sickness of Western society. As in the compassionate *Flight Into Camden* he would appear to stand for the sexual healing which was Lawrence's hope, for the healing of human relations which this demands, and not simply to be defiling in the de Sade manner that both consumes him and enrages him.

It is not possible to analyze every significant novel as closely. I must simply indicate where I think significance is to be found. Norman Mailer's *An American Dream* is a product of the same period. It appeared as a serial in *Esquire* in 1963–64, written in the appropriate overpunched language of the synthetic American thriller. Its theme is murder and sex, and the virility and excitement which comes from the combination of both. Rojack kills his wife and throws her off the balcony of a skyscraper apartment. She was bad ("She was bad in death. A beast stared back at me. Her teeth showed . . .") and had been incestuously corrupted in childhood, and so on, whereas Rojack is tough, a Faust, sold to the devil. "Murder, after all, has exhilaration within it. I do not mean it is a state to entertain; the tension which develops in your body makes you sicken over a period, and I had my fill of walking about with a chest full of hatred and a brain jammed to burst, but there is something manly about containing your rage, it is so difficult, it is like carrying a two-hundred-pound safe up a cast-iron hill. The exhilaration comes I suppose from possessing such strength. Besides, murder offers the promise of vast relief. It is never unsexual." [13]

It is inevitably part of the task of the novelist to invite us to identify with one or more of his principal characters. *An American Dream* presents only one dominant male, Rojack, who fills the stage. But he murdered his wife, lied to the police and got away with it. The novel caused a storm of controversy in the United

States. It seemed as though murder had been justified as a way of life—to which Mailer replied unambiguously in an interview: "I don't think anyone ever condemns murder *really*. Society may be founded on Kant's categorical imperative, but individual murder gives a sense of life to those around the event. Take newspaper readers—doesn't the suburban commuter get a moment of pleasure on the subway reading about murder? Is he perverse or is it really something life-giving? I prefer the second view of man, the less bleak one. . . . I don't know about the social consequences, all I know is that a man feels good when he commits a murder—immediately after, that is. Have you ever seen soldiers coming back from a killing spree? They're happy. If I wrote any other way about it, it would be meretricious." [14]

But the point is, alas, that *the book* is totally meretricious.[15] The minor characters are finely drawn and credible, the American scene is sharp, but the major characters are inconceivable and Rojack himself another concession to the boring American redskin tradition that the male hero is violent, ruthless and sexy in a neon landscape. It was serialized in *Esquire* at the time that President Kennedy was murdered.

Jean Genet's *Our Lady of the Flowers* is yet another celebration of sex and murder. Jean Genet was born, an illegitimate child, in Paris in 1910. He never knew his parents and was brought up by the *Assistance Publique*. He was ten when sent to a reformatory for thieving. Thereafter followed the life of a tramp, thief, vagrant, pimp and male prostitute described in *A Thief's Journal*. He seems to have been imprisoned in every one of the European countries he visited in thirty years of underworld roaming. In France alone he had ten convictions for theft; his last brought him life imprisonment but he was pardoned by President Auriol and freed on the appeal of a group of writers led by Jean Cocteau, then became famous. He was canonized by Jean-Paul Sartre, and as Saint Genet became rich.

Our Lady of the Flowers is another vein of the sexual subculture moving into the dominant. It was a fantasy written in prison on the brown paper with which prisoners make bags. A prison officer noticed the manuscript in the prison cell, took it away and burned it. Genet rewrote it. Its eventual publication by Gallimard, the revelation of its superb prose and its scabrous contents brought Genet instant fame, a fame hardly sustained by subsequent works. No one knows how, in a life totally without education, Genet learned to write so magnificently.

Our Lady of the Flowers is more unashamedly than *Justine* a masturbation fantasy. Genet plunders his imagination as de Sade did, though with less hysteria, and pulls the blanket over his head in the darkness of his cell to secure solitary erection and orgasm. The whole story moves in dreamlike sequences, some comic, some tragic, some sourly perverse, from one occasion of phallus worship to another. That is the intention; writing it in the cell, instead of daydreaming it, fixed it in a living dimension of its own. But his is not the normal world of sex but entirely the homosexual under-world. No other world is known. Not only is sex always inverted but every other value is inverted—and celebrated without shame or reticence.

Killing is easy, since the heart is on the left side, just opposite the armed hand of the killer, and the neck fits so neatly into the two joined hands. The corpse of the old man, one of those thousands of old men whose lot it is to die that way, is lying on the blue rug. Our Lady[16] has killed him. A murderer. He doesn't say the word to him-self, but rather I listen with him in his head to the ringing of chimes that must be made up of all the bells of lily-of-the-valley, the bells of spring flowers, bells made of porcelain, glass, water, air. His head is a singing copse. . . .

To love a murderer. To love to commit a crime in cahoots with the young half-breed pictured on the cover of the torn book. I want to sing murder, for I love murderers. To sing it plainly. Without pretend-ing, for example, that I want to be redeemed through it, though I do yearn for redemption. I would like to kill. As I have said above, rather than an old man, I would like to kill a handsome blond boy. . . .[17]

Even the dedication of the book is to a murderer.[18]

Violence, death, ordure, sexual murder and every perversion are celebrated with even more frenzy in *The Naked Lunch* by William Burroughs,[19] for Burroughs adds heroin, morphine and LSD and any other drug available to the already explosive mixture. The book has the horror of the dream of evil from which it is impossible for the dreamer, impotent, fragmented, and depersonalized, ever to awake. Of this book, I will speak of only two episodes. First, the book gives several descriptions of a peculiar anal perversion. Second, it appears to be a medical fact that when a man is hanged the pressure of the rope on the spinal cord causes an erection and ejaculation. The deliberate hanging of naked youths to cause this condition and to exploit it homosexually and heterosexually might be considered the main or at least the more-than-once-repeated theme of the book, if its fragmented pages could be argued to have any other theme but the total dissolution of human consciousness in real or imagined bestiality. Almost literally it is sex as spiritual and physical death and every description which the Christian fathers give of sex as bondage to horror would appear thereby to be justified. If this is all man can live for, man is indeed lost.

The controversial (but powerful and ideologically influential) books I have mentioned—there are many more, and still more films—represent that other theme, over against healing, of which I spoke, the theme of absolute liberty to describe and even to celebrate *any* experience. They represent an effort to abandon the notion of healing (as impractical and unfair, for a man has a right to his perversions) in favor of the widening of the range of possible experiences. In fact the doctrine of sexual liberty has become itself an ideology—all experiences have equal value, but perverse experiences are more equal than others, because once they were condemned. It is perhaps not the decivilizing of sex that is being sought but the death of our civilization which is already being celebrated.

5

Many examples of the vulgar exploitation of sex come from current films. It is sad that D. H. Lawrence's own work has been outraged to make a sexual holiday of precisely the kind that he would recognize as doing "dirt" on sex. *The Fox* is one of his most superb short stories. It is placed in the period of the First World War. Two girls are together running, not very successfully, a broken-down smallholding. Their relationship is what today we would call lesbian, but by that term we would already be distorting it, for there is not the slightest hint of sexual relations between the two girls or even that they understand their condition. Indeed, strong as the bond is between them, their relations are spinsterish and awkward rather as girl friends might be in a women's army barrack. It is the psychical dependence between them, the dependence of the weaker on the stronger, the responsibility of the stronger for the weaker, which justifies their lives, and makes them good for each other. Lawrence delicately exposes it.

The fox of the story is the almost daily predator of the henroost; it is a symbol for the predatory young soldier who insinuates himself into the cottage and is quick to realize that his own future is made if he could marry one of the girls and become master of the smallholding. He seeks to dominate the situation and, half in love with the most masterly girl, March, and half calculating, proposes to her. But the bond between the girls is too strong for him and he realizes that he can succeed only if he gets rid of the unwanted girl. He partly understands and wholly fears the strength of their relationship. Chance gives him the opportunity, when felling a tree, to murder the timid, sharp, virginal, unwanted Jill. He marries the surviving March who now finds her life meaningless because responsibilities and initiatives have been taken from it and she is reduced to a passive, dependent role. In this miraculously sensitive piece of writing there is not a single overt sexual act of any kind, though the desires are all there.

The director of the film ostensibly based on it, Mark Rydell, has corrupted the whole story, turning it into a blue movie. March (Anne Heywood) is made to strip and masturbate before a mirror. The courtship of March and Henry is transformed from a halting, groping conversation into a moaning naked coitus. And you can have all the lesbianism you want for your box-office money. The film demonstrates the transvaluation of all values, but in the opposite manner in which Nietzsche meant it. The cynical exploitation by the box-office avant-garde of one of the finest of

Lawrence's stories is a mark of how far we have moved into a new sexual philistinism. The most subtle comment on this comes from Richard Schribel.[20]

One of the differences between an adult and a child is that the former knows when to leave some things unsaid. One of the differences between an artist and an ordinary mortal is that his ability in this area is especially refined. Movies that pretend to either adult or artistic status in dealing with sex must cultivate this decent modesty not out of prudery but out of the knowledge that the true drama of the sexual encounter often occurs not in the act of love itself but in the life that surrounds it, conditioning and creating its quality. Naked truth, literal and figurative, is often the biggest lie of all, disguising the creator's inability to recognize where the heart of the enigmatic drama lies and implying, too, that he knows all about a subject that is, finally, unknowable.

The cultural disaster symbolized by the books and films I have been discussing is difficult to expose because it is bedeviled by the issue of censorship. It inhibited Pamela Hansford-Johnson in her sensitive probe into the cultural sources of the Hindley-Brady child murders, *On Iniquity*. Censorship is bad because it limits the creative freedom of the artist, the argument runs (which obviously counts more than the life or death of a child or two here or there). But this is a false analysis. Censorship may be necessary but it is bad because it is a clumsy and indiscriminate *external* instrument. The proper source of censorship is in the artist's conscience and this must be supported by a cultural consensus.

But if censorship is unworkable, sifting out often the wheat and saving the chaff, a second line of retreat from responsibility is the contemporary argument that pornography and obscenity do no harm. Those who will respond to their appeal will be those only who are "made that way." The others will be untouched. It is the weak, perverse mind alone which will be triggered off, and anything could have done that, even an illustration of underwear in a clothes catalogue.

Gilliam Freeman frequently makes this kind of defense of pornography in *The Undergrowth of Literature*.

It has been suggested that pornography can create anti-social behaviour—indencency, rape and murder. This argument is, to say the
least, unproven. No pictures and books can match the fantasies of the
human mind and to a diseased mind pornography is irrelevant; the
sadistic murderer will commit his crime without the aid of pornography. If pornography is to have any effect at all, it is apt to be
beneficial, acting as a mental aperient, a transference of need from the
act to the image; at most it leads to onanism, which is innocuous
enough. . . . I defy anyone to prove that people become depraved and
corrupted by pornography. Excited perhaps, amused, sexually stimulated. So what? This results in no more than the excitement of an appetite, the selection of a stimulant as natural and as personal as the
choice of food. One man's meat, in fact, is another man's pornography.[21]

And in her final paragraph, apropos sex, violence and fetishism
in children's comics, she writes, with the same air of offhand dismissal:

If there is no danger in exposing children to the gratuitous violence
in comics—and the law apparently assumes that there is not—where
does one draw the line? Or does one? Perhaps the innocent eye of
childhood can gaze unaffectedly on the type of sadism portrayed in the
pornographic bookshops of Soho. A child, after all, can more easily
apprehend pain and suffering than various sexual acts and we happily
expose them even in pre-school years to pictures and carvings of the
Crucifixion. At any rate, I see a much greater potential danger in
censorship, for that, demonstrably, has not been very successful.[22]

In order to see where this argument by non sequitur leads us
we have to transpose it to another sphere. Take, perhaps, violence.
That reflective writer, Milton Shulman, asked whether television [23]
might not be the real assassin of Robert Kennedy. Its ubiquity, its
immediacy, its taste for the violent and sensational in fiction and
fact permeated American society.

The sheriff only prevails over the outlaw because in the long run he
can shoot faster than his adversary. The private detective is better with
his fists and ju-jitsu than the crook he is chasing. The plainclothes
officer has more physical courage and is better with a revolver than

the drug pusher. The men from U.N.C.L.E. have more ingenious ways of committing mayhem than their international rivals.

From the moment he can first perceive anything, the American child is subjected to this scale of moral values. You don't have to argue, to be persuasive, to be logical, to be compassionate, to be ethical to achieve your objects in this world. . . . The best way to defeat evil is to beat it to the ground or obliterate it.

The refutation of this by the argument that violence in the cultural media has no effect comes virtually to this: *The culture has no cultural consequences.* What the cultural media, the mass media, the books and films show forth changes nothing. The violent will be violent, the peaceful peaceful, the chaste virginal, whatever you say or do. However, this is another argument still, a culture which makes no difference is totally worthless, even nonexistent. The television executive who argued to a women's conference that violence on television made no difference would not put the same point to an advertising client, but exactly the opposite one. Let me be dogmatic. A culture is a culture because it makes all the difference.

On the day on which I wrote this I read Philip Toynbee's hopeful account [24] of the student revolts in Europe. He spoke of visionary generations which saw and felt so clearly about certain aspects of life and society that they changed human consciousness. For him, one such was the first generation of the romantic movement, another, the generation which came to maturity in the First World War. We could add to the list. There was an idealist, visionary generation which preceded the French Revolution, of which Rousseau was the mentor. The nihilist and social revolutionary visionaries of nineteenth-century Russia so changed cultural attitudes that they gave birth to the theories of violence and terror which have painfully spelled themselves out in our time. And a handful of young visionaries, under the compelling leadership of Jesus of Nazareth, so revised man's conception of himself that they altered the entire course of human history. Not only is a culture a powerful force in molding human behavior but it can be changed decisively, permanently, in new and unexpected directions. The uprising of German youth which supported Hitler and almost brought him to world victory reversed the course of history and our political and moral aspirations in significantly evil ways, with which we still have to contend. So too did Stalin's young generation. There are black visionaries as well as angelic ones. The murder-and-sadism visionaries of our time, prophets in the wake of the Marquis de Sade, might easily prove as black a generation as any other, permanently altering our valuation of other lives, our treatment of sex, our attitudes to sexual exploitation.

It is perfectly senseless to imagine that it could "make no difference." Every young person at least seeks to live according to the sexual mores of his generation. These will be influenced by, and will influence, the mass media. This is how great cultural movements spring into being. To argue for neutralism, noneffectiveness in a culture, except in a limited way, is a disservice to anyone who speaks or writes in the hope of being listened to. Indeed it is more, it is the lie invented to save the makers of the mass-media culture from responsibility. They would like both to influence people and to be absolved from the consequences of doing it. It is for this reason that our culture is schizoid, and that we may properly speak of its sickness, particularly its sexual sickness. The latest phase of capitalism, that it exploits, propagates and makes profit out of sexual sickness, is perhaps worse than its first because in this it has an ally not present in any phase of labor exploitation—the heart of man, open like the ear of Othello to the whisper of Iago.

6

All depends finally on the view one holds of man. If he is a creature of greatness and responsibility then he must be held accountable in the end for what he does, whether in the course of a war in Vietnam or Cambodia, or as a consequence of the sexual mores to which he gives his allegiance. It must be admitted that, though we live in an age of some of the greatest human achievements, a sense of greatness has not rubbed off on to the authors of them. On the contrary, men are diminished in stature by the scale of their own accomplishments and by the magnitude of the moral disasters of a century which has not yet run its course, or played its full hand. One has to brace oneself physically in contemplating what yet may be.

Man is diminished too by what he learns to think of himself, in the messages which come across through the mass media, or trickle vulgarized down to him from the academic researchers of the higher culture. From all that is done and said he might well conclude that he is a behavioral "thing" rather than a responsible being —one for whom moral acts have no more validity than immoral acts, if indeed a distinction can any longer be made between them. That really is the crux—whether man can understand what is moral and sustain his understanding in the shapes and norms of his society. It is no easy task even in societies far less crazy with tensions than our own. I think it was Peter Berger who wrote somewhere that it is easier to set up human cultures than to keep them going. Time erodes their insights and crumbles allegiance.

Can one briefly and in conclusion, and against the climate of the times, show why man has to accept his greatness, his responsibility, his moral nature? Just those characteristics which his literature and his sciences appear to deny him? And in *sex* too, over which all Western societies are slightly insane, unable to decide between loathing and idolatry?

Perhaps one can best understand man's predicament by seeing man as a historical being through and through, as I described him earlier. A bird, an insect or a rabbit is not a historical being, but a natural one. We, not it, decide its place in natural "history." It is a creature of powerful instinctual urges which it fulfills when time and place are favorable. For the rest it appears to move from moment to moment in an eternal present by which the past is swiftly obliterated. It "forgets" (if the verb is appropriate) the generations from which it sprang and, as they mature, the generations to which it has given birth. It "forgets" the generations compresent with it, with which it is mingling and mating, hence David Hume's puzzle about incest.

Man too forgets. He forgets his past deeds and those who have died. But he struggles constantly against forgetting. Indeed to forget and to remember only have meaning in a human dimension, nowhere else. Man refuses to allow his past to die and labors to unravel it down to the dawn of time. He preserves his history, he plans his future. It is the nature of his being to live always along the dimension of time, yet he is always seeking to overcome his subservience to it. He reaches further and further back and further and further forward in his effort to understand and to master events. One has to describe him as a decision-making animal. This would be in line with existentialist thinking which sees man as thrown his freedom and then compelled to decide what to do with it. But there it is, the more man reaches backward in time, the more he is forced to decide what his being is, the more he reaches forward the more he is forced to decide *what to do*. Not all of that decision making is moral but much of it will be in the sense that he will reach for results which are useful and not harmful, for those ends he has learned to consider good as against those which would be bad.

This is particularly the case with sexual acts. His own life begins in a sexual act in the past. In a sexual act in the present, if it is fertile, he creates the future. He can never wholly divorce his sexuality from the future, or dismiss his responsibility for the future. Decision making makes man responsible; responsibility compels man to be moral, or to try to be moral. That is the briefest possible summary of his dilemma. For the truth is that a man's actual sexual urges are not interested in morality but in fulfillment. As every man discovers for himself, and as every broken marriage or raped girl witnesses, a sexual impulse does not leap up glorious with a morality which serves the individual or the social good but with all the blindness of the amoral id.

Man has, as best he may, to stand aside from his own impulses and to scrutinize them in the light of the consequences which could flow from them along the time track. That is, he must censor them morally. There is no escape from this imperative no matter to what society one turns. We cannot discover man outside society. We cannot discover societies without sexual and other disciplines. The present demand for total permissiveness and the sacralization of obscenity has to be judged in the light of all the other values man holds dear. Man has to come to terms with his sex in the light of his cultural heritage and not in alienation from it.

The great task of our age is to be honest, literate and clear-sighted about sex, but to be disciplined too, in the face of our unprecedented freedoms. This way, and not in a messy promiscuity, human greatness lies.

NOTES

CHAPTER ONE

1. Mentor, New York, 1952.
2. Humanities Press, New York.
3. A survey in 1963 and 1968 by Dr. William Kind, a school medical officer of Leicestershire, of a "carefully selected sample of about 400 18-year-olds" produced the following answers to the question "Do you approve of pre-marital sexual relations?"

	1963		1968	
	Men	*Women*	*Men*	*Women*
Yes, with any consenting party	39	10	22	Nil
Yes, under special circumstances	50	48	75	66
No	11	42	3	34

The *Observer* report (February 9, 1969) said this: "Those who answered 'Yes, under special circumstances' were then asked to give examples of the kind of special circumstances they had in mind. In 1963, 'being engaged' was the ... example quoted ... by 80 percent of the men and 100 percent of the girls." Five years later these percentages had dwindled to 20 percent and 30 percent respectively. As to intercourse 33 percent of the men and 68 percent of the girls were prepared to risk it without contraceptives. At the time of writing Dr. Kind's survey is not yet published.

4. McGraw-Hill, New York, 1968.

5. In the interview quoted earlier Mary Quant spoke of the crotch as the erotic zone the modern girl provocatively asserted by her dress and stance.

6. "Diary of the Seducer," *Either/Or* by Sören Kierkegaard, translation by David F. Swenson and Lillian M. Swenson, Princeton University Press, Princeton, N.J., 1944, Vol. 1.

7. Ibid.

8. Charles Hamblett and Jane Deverson, *Generation X,* Fawcett, New York.

9. Included in *Going to Meet the Man,* Dial, New York, 1965.

10. In the essay "Fable," *The Hot Gates,* Harcourt, Brace & World, New York, 1966.

11. Penguin, Baltimore, 1965; cf. also his *Introduction to Moral Education,* Pelican, London, 1967.

CHAPTER TWO

1. Of course, what is physically irreversible may be psychologically rejected, as in forms of homosexuality. And there are cases of "change of sex" but these are superficial, not fundamental, even in a sense fraudulent. The male changed into a "female" does not become able to conceive and the female changed into a "male" could not make a female fertile.

2. In "In Memory of Ernst Toller."

3. *Alternatives to Christian Belief,* Hodder & Stoughton, London, 1967.

4. It is commonly accepted that the Hitler regime massacred six and a quarter million Jews. Robert Conquest has worked it out that twelve million Russians died in labor camps (1933–50) and another eight million were victims of forced collectivization: twenty millions altogether! (*The Great Terror,* Macmillan, New York, 1968.)

CHAPTER THREE

1. Op. cit., Book III, Part 1, Section 1.
2. Royal and sacred incest is often cited as though it proved that incest, historically, has been common and acceptable and that modern censure of it is without justification. But as I wrote in *Nature Into History* the parallel is with murder as a private enterprise and as a political or religious act. "Human sacrifice, as a solemn religious theme, is the subject of the whole of *The Golden Bough,* but no one imagines that in societies where ritual human sacrifice was periodically performed, non-sacred murder was equally honored as within the law." The same must be true of incest. See the account of politically dictated incest in *The Golden Bough* by Sir J. G. Frazer, Abridged Edition, Macmillan, New York, 1949.
3. Op. cit., London, 1928; Peter Smith, Magnolia, Mass.
4. Ibid.
5. Op. cit., George Routledge, London, 1929; Harcourt, Brace & World, New York.

CHAPTER FOUR

1. A. J. Toynbee, *Study of History,* abridgement of Vols. I–VI by D. C. Somervell, Oxford University Press, New York, 1947.
2. Baldwin Spencer and F. J. Gillen, *The Northern Tribes of Central Australia,* Humanities Press, New York, 1966.
3. *Brown Men and Red Sand,* Tri-Ocean, San Francisco, 1967.
4. *The Northern Tribes of Central Australia.*
5. *The Stone Men of Malekula,* Macmillan, Toronto, 1942.
6. Gen. 17: 10–14 (R.V.).
7. Op. cit., Routledge & Kegan Paul, London, 1954; Pantheon, New York, 1954.
8. Ibid. For an eyewitness account of girls' initiation ceremonies among the Bemba of Northern Rhodesia, and their relation to sexuality and marriage, the reader is referred to *Chisungu* by Audrey I. Richards, Humanities Press, New York.
9. Dr. George Harley, "Notes on the Poro in Liberia," *Peabody Museum Papers,* Vol. 19, No. 2, Cambridge, Mass.; from *Reader*

in General Anthropology, C. S. Coon, Holt, Rinehart & Winston, New York, 1948.

10. Op. cit., translation by James Kirkup, Collins, London, 1955; Farrar, Straus & Giroux, New York, 1969.
11. Ibid.
12. Ibid.
13. *The Northern Tribes of Central Australia.*
14. Ibid.
15. Gen. 18: 17–18 (R.V.).
16. Lev. 26: 16 ff. (R.V.).
17. John Murray, London, 1952; under the title *We Chase the Islands,* William Morrow, 1952.

CHAPTER FIVE

1. Cf. *Alternatives to Christian Belief,* Chapter 9, "The Writer and the Human Condition."
2. *The Transition from School to Work,* Industrial Welfare Society, London, 1963.
3. Macmillan, New York, 1966.
4. Hodder & Stoughton, London, 1968.
5. Braziller, New York, 1957.
6. *Europa vor der Deutschen Frage,* Francke, Bern, 1946.
7. Panther, London, 1959.
8. A B.B.C. program spoke of ten thousand professional prostitutes at work in London's West End and estimated an annual turnover exceeding seventy million pounds.
9. In *Christian Century,* August 3, 1966; subsequently republished in *Sex is Dead,* Seabury Press, New York, 1967.
10. Issue of September 7, 1966.
11. Penguin, Baltimore, 1964.
12. Beacon Press, Boston, 1968.
13. Op. cit.
14. "Experimental Genetics and Human Evolution," issue of October, 1966, pp. 4 ff. In a clear, popular way Gordon Rattray Taylor covers the field of biological possibilties in *The Biological Time Bomb,* World, New York, 1968.
15. W. B. Saunders, Philadelphia, 1948.
16. Harper & Row, 1967.

17. In *The Annihilation of Man,* London, 1944; New York, 1945.
18. April 9, 1967.
19. Ibid., my italics.
20. How wrong all the prophets will then be! Down from Mary Shelley's Frankenstein to Capek's Rossum's Universal Robots and Dr. Who's Daleks and Cybermen in our own day, it was always assumed that the automata men built would turn out to be devils.
21. University of Toronto Press, Toronto, 1965.
22. Harcourt, Brace & World, New York, 1967.
23. November 10, 1967.

CHAPTER SIX

1. This is a shade too sweeping. In nursing, child care, teaching, midwifery, food services, etc., women would seem to find some gender fulfillment. All tough, physically exacting, aggressive occupations display male gender, the more particularly if they have an element of exhibitionism in them.
2. Pantheon, New York, 1960.
3. This despite the countermovement in Christianity, a Pauline movement to denigrate women because of their sex.
4. Harcourt, Brace & World, 1967.

CHAPTER SEVEN

1. Delacorte Press, New York, 1970.
2. Norton, New York, 1964; Penguin, London, 1965.
3. Penguin edition.
4. Published in *Sigmund Freud, A General Selection,* edited by John Rickman, Doubleday (Anchor Books), New York, 1957.
5. From personal observation when shopping I have noticed that the babies in prams are most likely to throw out their toys the moment that mother leaves them at the shop entrance and disappears inside.
6. A case of compensatory play came to my notice some years ago. A deeply disturbed little boy, deprived of his mother to whom he was greatly attached, rocked himself to sleep every night. This be-

havior became so compulsive that he continued it during sleep, causing his bed to travel around the room during the night.

7. Op. cit., Penguin edition, p. 211.
8. William Morrow, New York, 1949.
9. Margaret Mead and Martha Wolfenstein, University of Chicago Press, 1955.

CHAPTER EIGHT

1. It is a two-way love. Mary Miles (*Observer,* July 30, 1967) in an article entitled "Painful First Love" wrote evocatively of childish love, as in this moving passage: "I watched a little boy of just over two years meeting his mother after they had been separated while she was in hospital having her second child. He stood and looked and looked at her face with tremendous intensity as though he was relearning the loved features he had known so well before she left him: he put out one hand and gently touched her hair: he felt her face delicately with his finger-tips again and again; finally an ecstatic smile broke over his face and he went to her arms. Here, surely, was passionate love.

"He had been in the care of a devoted foster-mother and had shown every sign of confidence in her, yet at times in the middle of hugging her, he would attack her, scratching and biting because she was not the loved mother. Once when she sang to him, he said, 'No, don't sing, my mummy sings to me.'"

2. Norton, New York, 1964; Penguin, London, 1965.
3. International Documents Service, Columbia University Press, New York.
4. *Clinical Theology,* Humanities Press, New York, 1966.
5. Op. cit., Chapter 2 especially.
6. Cf. particularly *Centuries of Childhood* by Philippe Ariès, Knopf, New York, 1962.
7. CF. *My Dear Timothy,* Simon and Schuster, New York, 1953; *More for Timothy,* Gollancz, 1954; *Reminiscences of Affection,* Penguin, Baltimore, 1968.
8. *Reminiscences of Affection.*
9. Op. cit.
10. Ibid.
11. N. M. Iovetz-Tereshchenko, Allen & Unwin, London, 1936.
12. Op. cit.

CHAPTER NINE

1. Luke 11:5 ff. The parable tells of a friend at midnight who comes to borrow three loaves and gets the reply, "Trouble me not: the door is now shut, and my children are with me in bed; I cannot rise and give thee."

2. Gen. 3: 10–11 (R.V.).

3. *A Sailor Hat in the House of the Lord; the Autobiography of a Rebellious Victorian,* Allen & Unwin, London, 1967.

4. *Portuguese Voyages 1498–1663,* edited by Charles David Ley, Dent, Dutton (Everyman's), 1947.

5. October 27, 1967.

6. Faber, London, 1946.

7. "In the wave of earnest attempts to sweep away some of the taboos that were no longer appropriate to a society which had changed radically since they were developed, recently in the United States there was an epidemic of parents' attempts to protect their children from some of the misconceptions that psychoanalysis had discovered in neurotic patients by letting their children see them nude. When the next crop of neurotics, this time small children, reached the consulting-room, a new alarm was set up, because the clinicians reported that this was not necessarily the panacea it had been expected to be, that children were still frightened and confused and unaccepting of their sex. These well-meaning reformers had missed a serious link in the chain of learning. What the small child receives in a primitive society, and what he is coming closer and closer to receiving on our bathing-beaches today, is the assurance that there is a continuous series of steps between his small body and that of an adult." Margaret Mead, *Male and Female,* Morrow, New York, 1949.

8. Cf. *There was a Young Man,* H. M. Burton, Geoffrey Bles, London, 1958, p. 134. The young Burton has just joined the Army: "Before I reached the sergeant, however, I had been medically examined, and I shall not easily forget what I saw. There were a number of men and boys undressing in the same room with me and for the first time in my life I saw the adult male of the working class in all his nakedness. It was a warm day and my experience of the Langford-Road boys should have prepared me for the smell. I must have forgotten it. I had seen the grey dirty skins of

poor boys before, through holes in their trousers; but that their skins should have been that colour all over, and their feet black— literally jet black—was an additional shock. Open sores, bulging hernias, fantastically pendulant testicles—all these were novel and disgusting. Had I not given in my name and waited for an hour or more for the Army to realise that I was impatient to join its ranks, I should most certainly have turned and fled. I felt sympathy for the doctors, and a certain pride that they would at least have one clean body to deal with."

CHAPTER TEN

1. Grove Press, New York, 1962.
2. I explored the ambiguity of man's relation to, and his ignorance of, his body, in *Persons and Perception,* Humanities Press, New York, 1961.
3. Harcourt, Brace & World, New York, 1967.
4. In *The Hot Gates,* Harcourt, Brace & World, New York, 1966.
5. Op. cit., translation by Grace Frick, Secker & Warburg, London, 1955; Farrar, Straus, New York, 1963.
6. Op. cit.
7. From "Requiem," Robert Louis Stevenson.

CHAPTER ELEVEN

1. *The Viking Portable World Bible,* Viking Press, New York, 1939.
2. *Selections from the Notebooks of Leonardo da Vinci,* World's Classics, Oxford University Press, New York, 1952.
3. Op. cit., Harcourt, Brace & World, New York, 1959.
4. Into another kind of small boy, in fact, which is not surprising in a homosexual age. Many teen-age female sexual fashions deliberately exploit the small-boy, the *gamin,* resemblance.
5. *Living with Sex: The Student's Dilemma,* Seabury Press, New York, 1966.
6. Ibid.
7. But not just the moderns, of course! *Obscenity* is born out of contempt for the process and obscenity is universal.
8. *Lady Chatterley's Lover,* Grove Press, New York, 1962.

9. Ibid.
10. *Psychopathia Sexualis,* G. P. Putnam's, New York, 1965.
11. Donald J. Holmes, *The Adolescent in Psychotherapy,* Little, Brown, Boston, 1964.
12. Cf. *Persons and Perception,* Humanities Press, New York, 1961.
13. Translation by Paul Britten Austin, Little, Brown, Boston, 1963.
14. V. A. Demant, in *Christian Sex Ethics,* Harper, New York, 1965, traces the Christian responsibility for this.

CHAPTER TWELVE

1. From a review of Trigant Burrow's *The Social Basis of Consciousness* (1927), Phoenix (1936). I take the quotation from Sir Herbert Read's contribution to *Does Pornography Matter?,* Routledge & Kegan Paul, London, 1961.
2. Op. cit., Faber, London, 1929.
3. It is well, of course, to remember that aspect of Lawrence's philosophy which we all detested in the thirties, since it supported the pretensions of Hitler and National Socialism. Bertrand Russell quotes him in Volume II of his *Autobiography* (Atlantic Monthly Press, Boston, 1968): " 'There is' he [Lawrence] said, 'another seat of the consciousness than the brain and the nerves. There is a blood consciousness which exists in us independently of the ordinary mental consciousness. One lives, knows and has one's being in the blood, without any references to nerves and brain. This is one half of life belonging to the darkness. When I take a woman, then the blood precept is supreme. My blood-knowing is overwhelming. We should realise that we have a blood-being, a blood consciousness, a blood soul complete and apart from a mental and nerve consciousness.' " Russell thought this rubbish and said, "I did not then know that it led straight to Auschwitz." The value of "the blood-soul" in "taking a woman" is that it asks no questions, and "sacralization" too takes sex out of the ordinary rules of life. Lawrence could not abide the ordinary rules, but was quite ready to impose his rules on ordinary people.
4. Mellors, too, is the typical Lawrentian solitary—present gamekeeper, ex-miner, ex-ranker-officer, self-educated man—not a monster, but a sad outcast, he stands out from his society like a sore thumb.

5. In *Does Pornography Matter?*

6. Ibid.

7. "The Literary Censorship in England," Vol. XXIX, No. 115, June, 1967.

8. A urinal wall, covered with graffiti, in an English lavatory, bore the inscription at the foot, "This wall is available in paperback."

9. Alan Hull Walton's introduction to his translation of *Justine*, Corgi, London, 1965.

10. *Justine*.

11. Meridian, New York.

12. David Storey, *Radcliffe;* Coward-McCann, New York, 1964.

13. Op. cit., Dial Press, New York, 1964.

14. Interview with David Leitch, *Sunday Times* (London), April 25, 1965. I drew attention to these remarks in *Alternatives to Christian Belief*. Mailer was Robert Kennedy's friend and praised him after his assassination. Presumably his doctrine of the acceptability of murder was intended to except Mailer himself and at least his closest friends, just as those who justify incest would rather it were not practiced in their own homes. The Mailer of this book seems not only a poorer author but a different person from the author of *The Deer Park* and *Armies of the Night*.

15. I think Mailer's meretriciousness comes out in a flashback in which Rojack is made to relive a battle episode involving an attack on a German machine-gun post. "I was exploded in the butt from a piece of my own shrapnel, whacked with a delicious pain clean as a mistress' sharp teeth going 'Yummy' in your rump, and then the barrel of my carbine swung around like a long fine antenna and pointed itself at the machine-gun hole on my right where a great bloody sweet German face, a healthy spoiled overspoiled young beauty of a face, mother-love all over its making, possessor of that over-curved mouth which only great fat sweet young faggots can have when their rectum is tuned and entertained from adolescence on, came crying etc. etc." Who is making these sexual encyclopedia-like comments? Rojack, in the midst of the battle? Beyond belief! He could not possibly know, anyway. No, it is the author, not Rojack, speaking, so that the reader may be instructed how tough, brutal, ruthless, sexually omniscient, etc. etc., the *author* is.

16. All the male sexual inverts described by Genet bore flowery feminine names.

17. Op. cit., translation by Bernard Frechtman, Grove Press, New York, 1963.

18. The critics "come padding after . . . in . . . great, black, lunatic footsteps," Philip Toynbee remarked (*Observer,* March 24, 1968), demonstrating his theorem with two quotations from Richard Coe, *The Vision of Jean Genet* (Grove Press, New York, 1968). 1. "To reject the world, the most effective way (perhaps, when all is said and done, the *only* effective way) is to act in such a manner as to force the world to spew one out—in which case, Hitler came 'nearer to God' than St. Joan, St. Theresa or Vincent or Paul . . ." 2. "The Lover who sordidly betrays the object of his love for cash becomes the symbol of the metaphysical tragedy—and strangely, of the greatness of Man."

19. Grove Press, New York, 1962.

20. *Life,* May 13, 1968.

21. Op. cit., Delta Books, New York, 1970.

22. Ibid.

23. "Is *Television* the Real Assassin?" *Evening Standard,* June 12, 1968.

24. *Observer,* June 23, 1968.

INDEX

Abortion, 31, 34, 86
Abraham, 65–67
Affectlessness, 74–75
Aggression, 68, 109, 129
Alienation, 70–92
Alternatives to Christian Belief, 148
American Dream, An (Mailer), 164
Animals, 31, 49, 65
Annihilation of Man, The, 89
Anomie, 25
Anxiety Makers (Comfort), 103
Appetites, 35–37
    sexual, 13, 142–49
Aristotle, 11–12
Armytage, W. H. G., 91, 92
Atomization, inner, 74–75
Auden, W. H., 28
Augustine, St., 149
Australian aborigines, 51–54, 68, 120

Baldwin, James, 21
Berger, Peter, 173
Bernard, St., quoted, 149
Bible, 54, 66–67, 78
Birds, 28, 32, 49–50

Birth control, 31, 34, 56
Body, 131–42, 148
    adornment of, 48–49
    engineering of functions, 82–83
    privatization of functions, 120–22
Bonhoeffer, Dietrich, 78
Born Free (Adamson), 94
Bowlby, John, 112
Brady, Ian, 147–48, 162
Brill, Earl H., 77
Brothels, 102–3

Cannibalism, 36
Capitalism, anti-sexualism of, 97–98
Castration, 55–56
Censorship, 156–57, 169
Chateaubriand, François de, 161
Children, 103–8, 110–19, 125–28
Christ, 67, 171
Christianity, 70, 72
    sex and, 78
    sexual protests of, 149
    unlawful eroticism and, 102
    women and, 96
Circumcision, 51–66

Clones, 85, 91
Clothing, 130
  privatization and, 122–24
Coitus, 86–88
  in marriage, 102–3, 143
  romantic love and, 150
  spirituality of, 154–56
Comfort, Alex, 103, 111
Commodity
  labor as, 72
  sex as, 76–78, 109
Computers, 90–91
Crisis for the Humanities (Plumb),
  82
Cruelty, 21
  circumcision and, 64–65
  in play, 134
  See also Perversion
Cultural aggression, 68
Cybernation, 80–81

Dark Child, The (Laye), 59–61
Death, rebellion against, 140–42
*Death and Resurrection of the
  Church, The*, 72
Decision making, 81–82
Deviants, 73
  See also Perversion
Disciplines, 35–37
  of children, 111–12
  food and, 105–6
Distancing of the body, 131–39
  privatization and, 121
Division of labor, 80
Doctor Glas (Söderberg), 148–49
Dr. Zhivago (Pasternak), 88

Economics, of family, 101–2
  of gender roles, 93–97
Education, functional, 82
  sex, 125–27
Ego, development of, 106–7
Eickhoff, Louise, 125–26
Either/Or (Kierkegaard), 19
Erikson, Erik H., 106–7, 112, 113,
  133
Eroticism, 102
Evolution, 89, 91
Excretory functions, 104–5
  privatization and, 120–21

Exteriorization, 112–14

Family, 100–9
  gender roles and, 96–97
  incest and, 44
  nurture and, 32
Fantasy
  in play, 133–34
  pornography as, 159–60, 166
Federation of Progressive Societies
  and Individuals, 152–53
Female consciousness, 57
Fetichism, 145, 146
Fox, The (Lawrence), 167–68
Free Fall (Golding), 143
Freeman, Gillian, 147, 169–70
Freud, Sigmund, 22–24, 35, 49–50,
  73, 151, 154
  on circumcision, 55
  on incest, 39, 44
  on infantile sexuality, 106, 107
  latency and, 118
  on psyche, 37
  Sade and, 159
Friendship-Love in Adolescence
  (Iovetz-Tereshchenko), 117
Functionalism, 79–81
  reproduction and, 86
  scientific research and, 87–88

Gender roles, 27–29, 76, 93–97
  identity and, 25
  learned by children, 111
  social stability and, 152
Genet, Jean, 165–66
Genetics, 84–85
Gillen, F. J., 51, 53, 55, 61
God
  circumcision and, 54, 65
  sexlessness and, 78
Golding, William, 23, 135
Gollancz, Victor, 115–17
Grimble, Arthur, 67

Hannah, Pierce, quoted, 157
Hettlinger, Richard, 144
Hobbes, Thomas, 44, 49, 50
Hoggart, Richard, 155
Homosexuality, 145–46
  in novels, 162–63, 166–67

Horror, sexual, 148–49
Human Guinea Pigs (Pappworth), 83
Human Sexual Response (Masters and Johnson), 77, 88
Hume, David, 38–39, 47, 173

Id, 106–7
Identity, 25–26
  tribal, 54–55
Imprinting, 146
In Cold Blood (Capote), 75
Incest, 38–47, 104
Infanticide, 56
Infantile sexuality, 106, 107
  latency and, 118
Initiation ceremonies, 48–69
Instinct Sexuel, L' (Feré), 146
I.Q., 82

Jaurés, Jean, quoted, 110–11
Johnson, Virginia E., 77, 87, 88
Joad, C. E. M., 153
Jung, Carl, 73

Kerr, Clark, quoted, 92
Kierkegaard, Sören, 19–20
Kinsey, A. C., 22, 87–88, 144, 147
Krafft-Ebbing, Richard von, 21, 22, 146, 159

Labor, 72–73
Lady Chatterly's Lover (Lawrence), 131, 137
  trial of, 154–57, 160, 161, 164
Lake, Frank, 112
Latency of children, 112–18
  distancing of body during, 133–34, 139
  Oedipal stages and, 111–12
  significance of clothing during, 130
Lawrence, D. H., 131, 137, 145, 154
  exploitation of works of, 167–68
  sacralization of sex by, 154–56, 160
Layard, John, 53–54
Laye, Camara, 59–61
Leach, Edmund, quoted, 100

Lederberg, Joshua, 84–85
Legalization of sex, 102–4
Leonardo da Vinci, 141–42
Lesbianism, 168
  See also Homosexuality
Lions, gender roles of, 94
Love, parental, 45–46
  romantic, 149–50

McLuhan, Marshall, quoted, 77
Mailer, Norman, 164–65
Male consciousness, 57
Malincwski, Bronislaw, 40–43, 45
Malthus, Thomas, 30, 86
Man Makes Himself (Childe), 12
Marcion, quoted, 149
Marriage, 102–4, 143, 153–54
Marx, Karl, 72, 111, 153
Marxism, 90, 91
Masters, William H., 77, 87, 88
Masturbation, 103–4, 117, 146, 168
  fantasy for, 159–60, 166
Mead, Margaret, 40, 108, 128
Media, 170–72
Medical experimentation, 82–84
Memoirs of Hadrian (Yourcenar), 136
Men, 94–97
  sexual imperialism of, 143–44, 159
  See also Gender roles
Monogamy, 102, 104
  See also Pair bond
Morris, Desmond, 17, 95, 104, 121, 128, 138
Mountford, Charles P., 52–53
Mumford, Lewis, 92; quoted, 97
Murder, 39, 158–59, 164–67

Naked Lunch, The (Burroughs), 166–67
Nature into History, 12, 13, 44
Nazis, 89, 90, 110, 148
Nonsexual relations, 15–21, 22
Norms, reforms in, 153–54
Novels, pornographic, 158–67
Nurture, 31–32
  economics and, 102
  incest and, 44
  sexuality of children and, 108

Obscene Publications Acts, 156
Obscenity, *see* Pornography
Oedipus complex, 106, 118, 148
  cultural determinants, 151–52
On Iniquity (Hansford-Johnson), 169
Orgasm, research on, 87–88
Origins and History of Consciousness, The (Neumann), 56–57
Ortega y Gasset, José, 91
Osborn, Robert T., quoted, 78

Pair bond
  primitive, 138
  romantic love in, 150
  social stability and, 152
Parental love, 45–46
Péguy, Charles, 90
Perversion, 145–48
  exploitation of, 158–69
Philosophy, 89
  in pornography, 158–61
  of seduction, 19–21
Plato, 27–28, 30, 96
Play, 107, 133–34
Pornography
  as antisex, 154
  as exploitation, 75–77
  in films, 167–69
  philosophical, 158–61
  prosecution of, 156–57
  sexual subculture and, 163–67
Predators, sexual, 18–21
Privatization, 119–30
  of bodily functions, 120–22
  contribution to erotic life of, 136
  nakedness and, 122–25
  sex education and, 125–27
Promiscuity, 15, 31–32, 38
Property, 35–36
  family and, 102
Proprietory relationships, 32
Prostitution, 24, 27
  legal, 102–3
Puberty, 57–58

Quant, Mary, 15, 18, 77, 87, 130, 136, 150
Quarry (White), 134

Radcliffe (Storey), 162–64
Rais, Gilles de, 148, 160–61
Repression, 23–25, 50
Reproduction, 30–32, 98
  asexual, 29
  functionalism and, 86
  technology and, 84–85
Ritualization, 25
Robinson, John, 78, 155
Rolph, C. H., 157
Romantic Agony, The (Praz), 161
Romantic love, 149–50
Rousseau, Jean Jacques, 49, 171
Russell, Bertrand, 153, 184
Rydell, Mark, 168

Sacralization of sex, 154–56, 160
Sade, Marquis de, 22, 39, 158–61
Sandel (Stewart), 77
Sartre, Jean-Paul, 16–17, 165
Scarification, 54–55
Schenk, Ernst V., quoted, 74–75
Schribel, Richard, quoted, 169
Scientific research, 87–88
Secular City, The (Cox), 71–72
Secularization, 71–72
Seduction, philosophy of, 91–92
Sex education, 125–27
Sexlessness, 78, 98–99
Sexual appetite, 13, 142–49
Sexual signals, 129–30
Shulman, Milton, quoted, 170–71
Social Darwinism, 89, 91
Social stability, 152
Socializing of children, 110–11
Society
  bisexual nature of, 94–95
  ceremonies of initiation into, 48–69
  complexity of contemporary, 71
  functional, 79–81
  incest as threat to, 44
  property and, 36
  sexual activity in, 103–4
Söderberg, Hjalmar, 148–49
Spencer, B., 51, 53, 55, 61
Spengler, Oswald, quoted, 92
Sphincter control, 104–5
Spiritual imperialism, 68

Spirituality in coitus, 154–56
Stead, William T., 23–24, 103
Sterilization, 31
Storey, David, 162–64
Student revolts, 71, 171
Student sexuality, 144
Stylization, 25
Subincision, 55, 64
Sutherland, N. S., 90–91, 92
Symposium (Plato), 27, 96

Taboos, 39, 40–43, 45, 52
Technology, 70–92
    civilization and, 111
    gender role and, 97–98
    sexlessness and, 98–99
Teilhard de Chardin, 112
Tertullian, quoted, 149
Tom Sawyer (Twain), 133
Totem and Taboo (Freud), 49–50
Tower and the Abyss, The (Kahler), 74
Toynbee, Arnold, 68
Toynbee, Philip, 171
Tribal culture, 48–49
    bisexual order of, 94–95
    circumcision and, 51–54, 56–61
    nurture in, 108–9
Trobrianders, 40–43, 45, 104
Twenty Letters to a Friend (Svetlana), 88–89

Unlawful eroticism, 102

Vegetative propagation, 85
Victorianism, 102–3
    prostitution and, 24
    repression and, 23–25
    reversal of, 153, 157
Violence, 170–71
    See also Murder
Virility, circumcision and, 56–57
Vishnu Purana, quoted, 141–42
Voltaire, 159

Walton, Alan, 159
Wealth of Nations (Smith), 80
Well of Loneliness (Hall), 156
Wilson, Edmund, quoted, 161
Wilson, John, quoted, 25
Women
    Christianity and, 96
    consciousness of, 57
    economic role of, 94–97
    romantic love and, 149–50
    sexual appetite of, 143–45
    Victorian, 23
    See also Gender roles

Young
    nurture of, 31–32
    slaughter of, 33–34
    See also Children